INFORMATION TECHNOLOGY IN 21ST CENTURY

INFORMATION TECHNOLOGY IN 21ST CENTURY

(In 9 Volumes)

INFORMATION TECHNOLOGY
Threat to Freedom of Expression
(Volume 6)

PROF. RAMESH CHANDRA
Vice-Chancellor, Bundelkhand University, Jhansi (U.P.)

Publication

KALPAZ PUBLICATIONS

DELHI–110052

INFORMATION TECHNOLOGY IN 21ST CENTURY
Information Technology: Threat to Freedom of Expression
(Information Technolgy)

Rs. 8000 (Set)
Rs. 900 (each volume)

ISBN: 81-7835-158-7 (Set)
ISBN: 81-7835-164-1 (Vol. 6)

Published in 2003 in India by
Kalpaz Publications
C-30, Satyawati Nagar
Delhi-110052
E-mail: kalpaz@hotmail.com

Laser Typesetting at: A.S. Printers
Printed at: Chawla Offset Printers, Delhi

Preface

The internet is composed of a number of different ways of organizing, transmitting and accessing data. Because of this multiplicity of systems, it is unlike any other single medium. Rather, it incorporates characteristics of several other media and communications systems, including print, broadcast, and postal systems. Electronic mail allows for one-to-one or one-to-many communication. Gopher sites provide text-only information arranged according to menus. The World Wide Web allows for the display of many types of information, including text, images, sound and video, as well as interactive communication.

Expression via the internet includes the use of means that are private and others that are public. E-mail is private in the sense that the sender specifies the persons and addresses to whom it will be sent. By contrast, launching an open-access web site or posting a comment in a public newsgroup are acts of public speech since they are viewable by anyone who wishes to visit the web site or newsgroup.

Internet communication is highly vulnerable to surveillance and interception. A government agency can violate the privacy of e-mail correspondence just as easily as it can tap a person's telephone in order to listen to conversations or intercept faxes. The equipment needed is neither costly nor complicated to operate. Authorities can monitor by tapping an individual phone line and intercepting data streams as they are sent and received. If a user has internet access via a private ISP, employees of that ISP can open and read e-mail sent through it or allow police investigators to do so, unless special safeguards are put in place to protect privacy. If authorities have access to an ISP's server or the country's telecommunications network, they can capture e-mails while they are in transit.

Computer users have various means to protect their privacy and anonymity, some more effective than others. At the low-tech end, a user can try to avoid surveillance by using a computer terminal or e-mail account that is not being monitored, for example, one belonging to a friend. These techniques may help users escape identification if they are not already under surveillance, but they are no insurance against interception if a user's computer communication is being monitored.

This book attempts to analyse the threats of freedom of expression in the cyberspace and find out the proper legal framework to regulate them. Written in a lucid style, it attempts to provide proper guidance to computer professionals, academics, researchers, and students.

Editor

Contents

1

Freedom in Cyberspace

This chaper focuses on the latest Hungarian legal regulations from the aspect of the needs of the information society, and in particular the Internet. Authors' works form a great part of the information accessible on the Internet. The new Hungarian copyright act - based on recent international legislation regarding copyright in the Information Society - regulates free uses of authors' works as limitations of copyright.

According to the provisions of the act copying the work for private, educational or scientific purposes is considered to be a free use of the work, which may happen without permission from the author or paying royalty. Temporary (digital) reproduction also falls in the scope of free use on some conditions. These legal exceptions - based on the fair use-concept - are limitations of the author's exclusive rights in order to maintain a balanced regulation between the interest of authors and users of their works.

International background of the Hungarian Copyright Act

The WIPO "Internet treaties"

In 1996, when the need of creating an international basis for harmonized national legislation concerning copyright issues in the digital age became urgent, the diplomatic conference of WIPO (World Intellectual Property Organization) adopted two international treaties (currently signed by more than 50 countries of the world), the WIPO Copyright Treaty (hereinafter reffered as WCT) and the WIPO Performances and Phonograms Treaty (hereinafter reffered as WPPT).

The aim of the provisions of these treaties was to describe the uses of authors' works that takes place within and via Internet as a series of temporary and permanent reproductions and communications made directly or indirectly to the public.

Reproduction right

Before communicating (making available) a work to the public, it is needed to make a reproduction of it. WCT itself does not create a new notion of the reproduction right. Rather, reference is made to the relevant provisions of the Berne Convention , which are sufficiently broad to cover reproductions that take place in the digital environment.

The WPPT also states that: "The reproduction rights... fully apply in the digital environment. It is understood that the storage of a protected performance or phonograph in digital form in an electronic medium constitutes a reproduction within the meaning of these articles."

Communication to the public: the "umbrella solution"

WCT expands the Berne Convention's definition of "communication to the public" of works protected by copyright to include provisions for both perceptible and downloadable "transmissions" of works. According to the treaty: "authors of literary and artistic works shall enjoy the exclusive right of authorizing any communication to the public of their works, by wire or wireless means, including the making available to the public of their works in such a way that members of the public may access these works from a place and at a time individually chosen by them."

This definition - hopefully - covers all types of uses of the digital age (that's why it is often called "umbrella solution").

Limitations

The general consensus at the expert committee meetings and the diplomatic conference (leading to the adoption of WCT and WPPT in 1996) determined that the limitations and exceptions provided by the existing and newly-created exclusive rights should apply in the digital environment. The limitations and exceptions addressed by both treaties approach the subject from different directions. The delegates agreed that "the mere provision of physical facilities for enabling or making a communication does not in itself amount to communication within the meaning of WCT or the Berne Convention." As a result, the "mere conduit" may not constitute an act of communication (making available) to the public.

Both WCT and WPPT grant the contracting parties the freedom to provide new limitations or exceptions in their national legislation, and to extend existing ones to match the rights granted to authors of literary and artistic works under WCT . This freedom applies in cases where

- there is no conflict with a normal exploitation of the work, and
- the legitimate interests of the author are not unreasonably prejudiced.

A similar authorization under WPPT (using the same language in respect to the boundaries of the creation and extension of limitations and exceptions) applies with regard to the protection of performers and producers of phonograms .

The right of communication to the public in the new Hungarian Copyright Act

From the aspect of the new Hungarian copyright act (Act LXXVI of 1999, entered into force 1 September, 1999, hereinafter referred as CA), on-line uses of authors' works must be considered as a two-step procedure, the first step being placing (uploading) the work onto a server connected to the Internet. Based on the provisions of the WCT, the act qualifies this activity as communication of the work to the public , which must be licensed by the author (in Hungary this happens through extended collective management of rights).

The second step of the procedure is accessing (displaying, downloading) the work on the Internet by users, which phase is regarded - under certain conditions - as copying the work for private purposes, which - according to the regulations of the act - is considered to be a free use of the work, which may happen without the permission of the author or paying royalty.

Cases of free use in the Hungarian Act regarding on-line uses

Exceptions are limitations of the rightholder's exclusive rights. The role of these exceptions - so called free uses in the Hungarian law - is to maintain a balance between the respectable private interests in accessing information and the authors' interests in getting fair and equitable remuneration in return of the uses of his works. Among the cases of free uses described in the CA, the legislator - harmonizing with the recent relevant EU-provisions - included special cases regarding the latest technological possibilities of the information society (temporary reproduction of the work).

Private copies

Home copies

According to the Hungarian copyright act "a copy of the work may be made by anyone for private purpose if it is not designed for earning or increasing income eve in an indirect way. This provision shall not apply to (ÿ) software and databases operated by a computing device."

But the CA contains restrictions regarding literary works: "A complete book as well as the whole of a periodical or daily may be copied even for a private purpose only by handwriting or typing.."

Internal (institution) copies

The CA gives the opportunity to institutions (such as scientific institutions, libararies) to make internal copies of authors' works as follows:

- in a manner and to the extent complying with the intended purpose as well as for internal use in an institution, if it is outside the scope of commercial activity a copy may be made for own purposes if it is not designed for earning or increasing income even in an indirect way and

a) it is required for scientific research,

b) it is made from an own copy for the files to be used for scientific purpose or for the supply of a public library, or

c) it is made of a limited part of a published work or of an article in a newspaper or a periodical."

Copies in educational institutions

- Specific parts of a work published as a book as well as newspaper and periodical articles may be reproduced for educational purposes in a number corresponding to the number of pupils in a class or for purposes of exam in public and higher education in a number necessary for the said purpose."

Temporary reproduction

- The temporary reproduction of a work done with the exclusive purpose to permit the realization of the use of the work authorized by the author or permitted pursuant to the provisions of this Act shall be taken to fall within the scope of free use on the condition that the temporary reproduction is an integral part of the technological process aiming to achieve the said use and lacking any economic significance of its own."

These provisions enable users to access works by browsing, or with the help of search engines, and automatic caching. Mirror caching for example, as not being the integral part of the technological process aiming to achieve the free use, and may have independent economic significance, is not permitted without the licence of the rightholders upon this section of the CA.

Licensing in practice: collective administration of authors' rights in Hungary

According to the CA, licensing of different type of on-line uses of authors' works (such as streaming, webcasting or on-demand uses) in Hungary is done by the collective managing society (Artisjus) appointed by the Ministry of National Cultural Heritage.

The royalty-tariff chart (attached to this paper as Annex I.) regarding on-line uses (determined each year by Artisjus and approved by by the Ministry of National Cultural Heritage) has extremely detailed provisions concerning the new types of uses of works in the digital environment.

The tariff has many special regulations making differences between several types of communication to the public such as broadcasting-type (streaming and simulcasting) and on-demand uses (download, real audio).

Newly developed technological methods offer more and more possibilities to access information. Only a well developed, internationally harmonized legal system can constitute the balance required between the interests of users (accessing more and more information for free, without any legal obstacles) and of authors (getting equitable remuneration).

2

Threat to Freedom of Expression

Large companies have traditionally viewed any new media as a threat. Unconventional forms of publishing and speech challenge conventional ways of conducting business. Historically, only an exceptionally small and forward-looking group of companies take advantage of new media. Others resist their implementation, and attempt to use legal mechanisms to frustrate access to such technologies and techniques.

The recent moves by large industry groups and companies to inhibit free expression on the Internet is predictable. Attempts by the film and music industries to paralyse the development of new technologies of consumer content distribution is entirely consistent with their initial responses to photocopier and video technology.

This chapter assesses the attempts being made by these industries to curtail content and distribution on the Internet, and discusses the likely result of such moves.

The new battleground of free speech

Attempts by Western Governments to curtail free speech on the internet have largely failed. Internet censorship provisions in the US Communications Decency Act 1995 and the Child Online Protection Act 1998 have been struck down by the Supreme and Federal courts (Reno v. ACLU 1996; ACLU v. Reno 2000). While some other Western countries are still attempting to censor the net, it is likely that they will achieve little more than to drive the content of websites to First Amendment-protected US Web servers, where it is only a few milliseconds further away from their citizens.

Some governments, such as those of China and Singapore, have attempted to block certain content (most notably pornography and political commentary) from entering their countries by using firewalls and restricted connectivity. These efforts have not taken account of recent developments in Internet technology, and are likely to fail in the long term because of services that anonymise Internet activity. Any Internet user can connect to services such as anonymizer.com, which will make the task of monitoring and blocking virtually impossible. The growing use of encryption will compound the task of censorship. As Internet usage increases in those countries, the reliability requirements of e-business will also force better connectivity.

Future government attempts at censorship may centre around making Web hosts liable for the content they serve, similar in some respects to conventional publishing law. Britain has a "notice and take down" system as a result of a successful defamation prosecution by UK academic Lawrence Godfrey against the Demon Internet Service Provider (ISP) (Lawrence Godfrey v

Demon Internet Limited 1999). The US has a similar provision under the Digital Millenium Copyright Act 1998 with regard to copyrighted material. This latter effort is being driven by a new threat to free speech: big business.

The industry challenge

Notice-and-take-down laws have been largely driven by the music industry, which is demanding that ISPs not allow copyrighted MP3 music files (a compressed data format) to be distributed from their sites. Even MP3.com, who designed technology especially to allow users with legal copies of music to access it over the Internet, has been pursued through the courts by the big labels. The company has agreed to pay royalties to four of these companies, but may have to pay up to $250m to settle a lawsuit with Universal Music Group

New technology such as Napster has provoked an even more extreme response. The company, which provides an on-line community for the sharing of music, has faced a life-or-death court attack from the Recording Industry Association of America, currently awaiting a decision from the federal Court of Appeal in California.

The movie industry has also aggressively pursued those it claims are violating its copyright online. DeCSS, a program written to allow Digital Video Disks (DVD) to be played on Linux computers (an operating system that competes with Microsoft Windows), has been targeted on Web servers all over the world by the Motion Picture Association of America. The MPAA has attempted to obtain injunctions in New York and California courts to prevent the publication of or even linking to DeCSS.

These efforts to threaten ISPs extend even outside the jurisdiction of the US courts of law [Young1998]. One of the program's authors, 16-year old Jon Johanssen, was arrested at home in Norway and had his computer equipment seized.

The content industries have also expended substantial resources lobbying legislatures, particularly the US Congress, to pass new laws reducing citizens' "fair use" rights that allow limited non-commercial reproduction of copyright materials.

The US Digital Millenium Copyright Act has been heavily criticised for banning devices that allow circumvention of copyright control mechanisms even for these limited fair use purposes [Samuelson99].

Industry is heavily lobbying the US state legislatures to pass the Uniform Commercial Information Transactions Act, an update to the US Uniform Commercial Code that governs interstate commerce. This update gives powers to enforce information "licenses" that may exclude fair use rights [Samuelson98].

Various music groups have also been taking technical measures to try and stop the distribution of their music via services such as Napster.

Metallica and Dr. Dre both monitored Napster's servers to obtain lists of users making their songs available, and then demanded that Napster block those people's access. They then have the option to take legal action against any of those individuals.

A Xerox Parc study found that only a small percentage of file swappers made their own music files available to others [Adar00]: these people would be the obvious first legal targets.

Stopping whistleblowers

Various companies have used related technical and legal attacks to uncover the identities behind pseudonymous critics and whistleblowers. In many cases, ISPs will comply with corporate requests for information on their users without any judicial authorisation.

Companies have a long history of using telephone records to identify whistleblowers and other sources of embarrassing information.

They are now turning to Internet surveillance for the same purpose. Corporate mail servers may provide copies of e-mails sent and received. The addresses of Web pages visited by employees may also be logged. Many companies are eager to use these powers.

Governments are reluctant to provide protection against such measures. The United States has fought pressure both from its own citizens and from the European Union to pass privacy protection legislation. The United Kingdom has explicitly authorised employee monitoring for a wide range of purposes.

It has also provided powers for a large group of government authorities to obtain "traffic data" on Internet users' activities, and to require ISPs to store such data. This measure has the unintended effect that such information will be available to any organisation willing to bribe unethical individuals with access.

The US and UK law enforcement and intelligence communities have been prime movers in extending these powers to governments around the world via the Council of Europe's draft Cybercrime treaty.

New technologies

Napster and Gnutella (another popular file-sharing program) have different, but similarly damaging, flaws. Napster uses central servers to index the files available on its users' hard disks. These central points are easy targets for legal and technical attacks, as the record companies have been quick to realise. Gnutella identifies the source of any file downloaded, providing a target for prospective legal action.

The record industry has been attempting to prevent duplication of music through their Secure Digital Music Initiative. Their vision is of a world of music devices-CD players, walkmans, radios-that will refuse to allow copies of songs marked by their publishers as "not for copying". However, attempts to create the building blocks of these technologies have so far failed. Just one group of researchers broke all four of the candidate marking algorithms SDMI had selected. Due to fundamental problems in securing mass-market devices, SDMI is unlikely to succeed.

New file-sharing technologies designed to avoid the weaknesses of Napster and Gnutella are now becoming available to distribute these de-protected songs. Freenet uses a distributed search and copy mechanism that masks the identities of users and caches files so they are available quickly to users around the world.

Mojonation allows files to be split redundantly between several users: each split is hard to find, but even if removed can still be reconstituted from other splits if available. It also provides a micropayment mechanism that rewards users who make resources such as disk space available to the network, avoiding the problem of users willing to download but not share files, as identified by the Xerox study.

These new technologies are very likely to overcome the content industries' censorship attempts. Unfortunately the companies' determination to change the balance of copyright law in their favour may diminish many other conventional rights in the process. It would be tragic if the content industries adapted to new Internet business models, but left a legacy of restrictive laws before doing so. The business world moves far faster than the legal environment.

It is ironic that media companies have historically been some of the staunchest defenders of First Amendment rights. It would be unfortunate if this was now to change as their profits were threatened.

Copyright is a balance struck between society and authors, not an inalienable right of the copyright holder. The US Constitution allows Congress "To promote the progress of Science and Useful Arts, by securing for limited Times to Authors and Inventors the exclusive Right to their respective Writings and Discoveries." If society feels the benefits of copyright are flowing too heavily to intellectual property owners, it will slowly but surely start to move that balance back in its own direction. Legislators are influenced heavily by lobbyists, but even more by the prospect of large numbers of votes from citizens who may come to resent attacks on their freedom of expression.

Freedom of Expression on the Internet

Even as governments around the world acknowledged the difficulties inherent in censoring the Internet, legislative proposals continued to threaten free speech. While human rights and civil liberties groups pointed out the global implications for the rights to privacy and free expression represented by such proposals, regulators around the world were quick to refine online monitoring, screening, and other controlling technologies.

Arguing that national regulatory frameworks are not appropriate to the global nature of the Internet, industry leaders joined forces to create an international Internet content rating system to "protect children and free speech" on the Web. In May they formed the Internet Content Rating Association (ICRA) to facilitate the development of an integrated self-regulatory approach to dealing with "harmful and illegal" content on the Internet.

Human Rights Watch, along with other members of the Global Internet Liberty Campaign (GILC), argued for more deliberate consideration of so-called self-regulatory approaches to Internet content control. The Global Internet Liberty Campaign Member Statement (submitted in September to the Internet Content Summit) further emphasized the danger that rating and filtering systems could, in fact, facilitate government censorship.

The wide-scale deployment of rating and blocking systems could be used by regulators to stifle expression and marginalize any Web sites that failed to adopt ratings. The existence of a standardized rating system for Internet content-with the accompanying technical changes to facilitate blocking-would allow governments to require Internet service providers (ISPs) and other content access providers (public libraries, schools, etc.) to employ such regimes.

Exemplifying this possibility, the Australian government on June 30, 1999 approved the Broadcasting Services Amendment (Online Services) Act (scheduled to go into effect in 2000), which would force Australian ISPs to remove objectionable material from Australian sites and to block access to similar sites overseas. Material suitable for blocking was to be identified based on existing national film and video classification standards. The new law placed sweeping restrictions on adults providing or gaining access to material deemed unsuitable for minors.

In Bahrain, Iran, Saudi Arabia, the United Arab Emirates, and Yemen, ISPs-either under government orders or pressure-all blocked Web sites on the basis of their content. At least in the first four of these countries, blocking extended to cultural and/or political content. Proxy servers such as the ones in place in the U.A.E. and Saudi Arabia could be used by authorities to track which computer terminals were accessing which Web sites and for how long. While U.A.E. authorities denied monitoring individual Web use, Saudi Arabian users who requested blocked sites received a message on their screens warning that all access attempts were logged.

State-controlled or state-influenced ISPs in Tunisia, Iran and Bahrain blocked Web sites containing political or human rights criticism of their governments. Tunisia acknowledged blocking only those sites that offended moral values, but apparently this included the sites of various human rights organizations critical of the government.

Videsh Sanchar Nigam Ltd. (owned by the Indian government) was the nation's largest Internet service provider and controlled the international Internet gateways used by ISPs in India. During the last week of June, at the height of the Kashmir crisis, Internet users in India could not reach the online news site of the Pakistan daily Dawn, which was known for its independent coverage of the crisis. Fearing that VSNL gateways blocked access to the newspaper site, other Web sites began posting information explaining how surfers from India could break the blockade, and a number of mailing lists began circulating articles from Dawn in text format.

Radio B92, the leading independent radio station in Belgrade, Yugoslavia, was banned in March but continued to broadcast news on the Internet. Online users around the world were able to continue to access Radio B2-92's independent news via the Web as a daily digest with headline updates every hour.

In late 1998 the United States Congress passed the Child Online Protection Act (COPA), making it a crime to publish "any communication for commercial purposes that includes any material that is harmful to minors, without restricting access to such material by minors." In April the U.S. Department of Justice appealed a federal appeals court ruling declaring the law unconstitutional, the result of a lawsuit brought by opponents of the COPA.

Monitoring and Surveillance

Governments rarely admit to "eavesdropping" on e-mail, and it is extremely hard to ascertain whether government monitoring is occurring when most information about monitoring mechanisms is classified. But during 1998 official disclosures in Europe and Australia provided a glimpse into one such system, a monitoring process referred to as ECHELON. According to a January 1998 report published by the Scientific and Technological Option Assessment (STOA) unit of the European Parliament, ECHELON formed part of the UKUSA spy system and wasdesigned for primarily non-military targets: governments, organizations and businesses. The system operated in virtually every country and intercepted fax, e-mail and telephone messages routinely and indiscriminately.

In Britain, the Home Office announced a number of proposals in a June 1999 consultation paper on the interception of communications. Future laws based on these proposals would require "communications service providers" to integrate government interception facilities into their networks, including the Internet, at their own expense. These proposals followed the specifications secretly agreed by European police officials in ENFOPOL plans revealed the previous year. (ENFOPOL was a standard European Commission classification for documents concerned with law enforcement matters.) The British consultation paper also argued that the maintenance of an interception capability was a basic requirement for providers of communication services in countries such as France, Germany, the Netherlands, Sweden, Canada, the United States and Australia.

On April 2, the Second Chamber of the Dutch Parliament approved a new Telecommunications Act that included a chapter intended, among other things, to force ISPs to facilitate monitoring by the police and intelligence services.

In April, an Internet service provider, Singnet of Singapore, apologized to its subscribers after scanning their computers without their knowledge. Singnet had asked the Home Affairs Ministry to check the computers of its 200,000 subscribers during a computer virus scare.

In Russia rules requiring ISPs to provide the security service with complete access to users' e-mail were challenged by an ISP based in Volgograd. The rules, known as System of Efficient Research Measures 2 (SORM-2), were written by the Russian Federal Security Services and the State Communications Agency in 1998.

In the Middle East and North Africa, where many governments routinely tapped the phones of potential dissidents, Internet users in many countries, including Bahrain and Tunisia, suspected that the right to privacy of correspondence was being violated by government surveillance of e-mail communications. One Bahraini spent more than a year in jail on suspicion of e-mailing "political" information to dissidents abroad.

Under India's License Agreement Provision of Internet Service, ISPs had to maintain logs of all Internet users and the service they were using. These logs, as well as copies of all the packets originating from the customer premises equipment (CPE) of the ISP, had to be available in real time to the government telecom authority (in other words, the telecom authority had access to live communications).

According to BBC News Online, a Sri Lankan government minister admitted in August that he had intercepted a personal e-mail sent to the leader of the country's opposition.

China continued its crackdown on Internet dissent by explicitly prohibiting the transmission or posting of what the government considered "anti-government propaganda." In January 1999, a computer technician, Lin Hai, was sentenced to two years' imprisonment by a Shanghai court for giving the e-mail addresses of 30,000 Chinese subscribers to a dissident site that published an online magazine from the United States.

In a worrying development, Internet providers and telecommunications companies in many countries could be forced to build special data taps into their Internet servers to allow government security agencies real-time monitoring of every e-mail message and Web page sent to or from their servers. This could allow government agencies to circumvent national privacy laws (such U.S. laws that bar the government from spying on its citizens), allowing them to rely on surveillance mechanisms in other countries. Citing national security concerns, governments continued to avoid releasing information on monitoring mechanisms.

Encryption

The promise that the Internet held for human rights was limited by the fact that electronic communications were highly vulnerable to interception, with potentially deadly consequences for those who would expose abuses of state power. The development of and freedom to use encryption software could provide substantial protection for the privacy of online users. Yet contrary to the spirit of international norms that recognize privacy as a fundamental human right, governments continued to use export controls or other national laws limiting the public's access to encryption technologies and inhibiting the development of new encryption products. In December 1998, the Wassenaar Arrangement (a group of thirty-three states) announced, largely due to United States pressure, new guidelines that would authorize restrictions on the export of most commercial cryptography products above a fifty-six or sixty-four bit strength.

But there were other, more encouraging developments in this area. In Germany, as of September 1, an export license was no longer required for the export of encryption products to third-country markets. Ireland, counter to the wishes of its E.U. neighbors, was willing to adopt policies that favored the use of strong encryption to encourage Internet trading. The French prime minister announced in January that due to the threat of electronic espionage and other dangers to privacy France would allow encryption strengths up to 128 bits, and would remove the compulsory or third-party escrow of encryption keys.

As should be evident, the field of Internet regulation and surveillance was still very much in flux in 1999. It was clear, however, that the privacy and free expression rights of users of this global medium would be shaped by a multiplicity of regulations and policies, including self-regulatory approaches promoted by Internet industry leaders as well as myriad national and international rules on surveillance and encryption.

3

Information Systems Accountability

Increased accountability is a key component of public sector reform. This chapter investigates the relationship between accountability and both information technology and information systems. It concludes that IT has had a very mixed impact, supporting accountability in some cases, but also skewing or undermining it in others. Information systems—computerised or not—are an essential part of public sector accountability. However, new IS have a flexible impact, with accountability outcomes being determined mainly by management decisions and by wider organisational and environmental factors. As such, the broader context must be conducive to accountability before accountability IS initiatives will work.

The Context of Public Sector Reform

Public sector reform is, if generally defined, change within public sector organisations (PSOs) that seeks to improve their performance. As such, public sector reform has been an ongoing process since the inception of institutions that we might now label 'public sector'.

However, public sector reform is typically defined more narrowly. It is seen as a process that grew up particularly from the 1970s for which three overarching (and interlinked) causes may be identified.

Crisis in the public sector

If all had been well in the public sector, no consistent trend, let alone ideology, of reform would have emerged. However, a perception of problems with the public sector, even of crisis in some countries, emerged during the 1970s. The perceived problems were focused on:

— *Inputs*: In a number of countries, the public sector was seen to require unsustainably large and/or unsustainably increasing public expenditure.

— *Processes*: There was concern about examples of waste, delay, mismanagement and corruption within the public sector, all of which contributed to inefficiency in the conversion of public expenditure into public services. In particular, public servants were seen as sometimes making decisions in their own interests rather than in the interests of the public. That they were able to do so was seen as a twin failure. First, of centralisation, which made decision makers too remote from the locus of decision information and action. Second, of unaccountability, which made decision makers too remote from those outside the organisation who were affected by their decisions.

— *Outputs*: Finally, there was a perceived problem with outputs. Concerns were widespread in a number of countries that the public sector was not delivering what it should, from adequate defence and control of crime through support for agriculture and industry to health, education, housing, social welfare and a hundred other responsibilities.

The sense of difficulties came to cover both *what* the public sector was doing (the public sector's role) and also *how* it was doing it (public sector organisation and management).

If there had been no ideological peg on which to hang many of the trends of change within the public sector, reform measures would have been less clearly recognised and probably less strongly promoted. Such a peg emerged slowly after the Second World War and with gathering pace from the 1970s in the form of 'neo-liberalism'. Neo-liberalism is a resurgence in the ideas of liberalism that can be traced back to John Locke and Adam Smith in, respectively, the seventeenth and eighteenth centuries. It provides a substantial theoretical framework that can be used to justify a set of public sector reforms.

In its crudest form - 'market good, government bad' - neo-liberal thinking emphasises what it sees as the economic efficiency of markets and the forces of competition and individual decisions. It also emphasises what it sees as the inefficiency of governments and the forces of collective, planned intervention. Three particulars flow from this viewpoint:

— that, wherever possible, there should be a 'rolling back of the state'; in other words, the replacement of the state with privately-owned institutions

— that the main justification for the continued existence of the state is its role in helping markets to function more efficiently

— that, where state institutions remain, they should, wherever possible, be opened up to true or quasi-market forces of competition.

Neo-liberalism therefore had something to say not just about the role of the public sector, but also about the way in which it might be organised and managed.

Political will and power

A sense of crisis and an ideology of reform are necessary, but not sufficient conditions for reform. There must also be a third element: that of the political will and power to enact reform. Three main components of the political economy in most countries can be identified that influence this.

— *The populus at large* has often borne the brunt of public sector crisis, has typically longed for reform, but has had only limited political capacity to have those reforms enacted.

— *Politicians and public servants* have often been divided, with conflict between those supporting and those resisting reform.

— *Local and global capital* has sometimes been divided but has more generally sought reform in the belief that this will reduce business costs and increase transaction speed.

In some countries, particularly the developing and transitional economy countries, there has been a fourth component of political economy:

— *International organisations* have often been a powerful - sometimes the most powerful - driving force behind public sector reform. These agencies have the political power to pursue reform because many countries, struggling with both international trade and domestic spending deficits, have had to request external sources of financial assistance. Since the 1970s, such requests have often been met with 'conditionalities'. These are requirements by international finance organisations for changes in the recipient country's economic and institutional structures. In return for agreement to begin implementation of such changes, financial assistance is provided.

These agencies have the political will to pursue reform because they are largely driven by a neo-liberal agenda. Reform measures concerned with government policy include: removing trade barriers, encouraging foreign investment, floating the local currency, privatising government-owned enterprises, and so on. Other measures - often falling under the wider heading of 'good governance' - are basically those of public sector reform outlined below in section 1a, which aim to improve the internal workings of the public sector.

The political economy of every country is different. However, one stereotypical outcome of these various forces has been a process of reform that is driven largely from outside the public sector, whilst being resisted by at least some portion of public servants.

Components of Public Sector Reform

Where public sector crisis prompted the call "Something should be done", neo-liberal ideology provided the response "Something can be done" and, in some situations, political driving forces demanded that "Something will be done". This "something" has come in the form of various measures that fall collectively under the heading of 'public sector reform'.

There is no consistent menu of elements that make up a programme of public sector reform. Typical components, however, include:

— *increased efficiency*: improving the input:output ratio within the public sector; the rationale of such reforms is to address the large size of public sector expenditure and/or the inefficiency of many of its processes

— *decentralisation*: the transfer of decision making to lower, more localised levels of the public sector; the rationale of such reforms is to reduce the costs of centralised decision making, and to create more flexible and responsive decision making

— *increased accountability*: making public sector staff more accountable for their decisions and actions; the rationale of such reforms is to increase the pressure on staff to perform well, to make them more responsive to recipient groups, and to reduce corrupt practices

— *improved resource management*: increasing the effective use of human, financial and other resources; the rationale of such reforms is clear from their definition

— *marketisation*: increasing the use of market forces within the workings of the public sector; the rationale of such reforms is that market relations will drive costs down and increase efficiency and/or effectiveness.

In chapter paper, we will look at the third element: accountability.

Defining Accountability

The interest in accountability within public sector reform was defined above as a desire to make public sector staff more accountable for their decisions and actions. In more detail, this means:

— that some set of recipients receives information about the outcomes of decisions made by identified individuals who are source decision makers

— that those sources can be made to explain their decisions

— and that some sanctions can be imposed if the explanations are unsatisfactory.

But to whom should public servants be accountable? There is a broad set of accountabilities in the public sector, including:

— *Managerial accountability*: to senior managers within the organisation. For example, public servants may be held accountable by their immediate boss for their attendance record.

— *Political accountability*: to those institutions that provide the political legitimacy of the organisation. For example, PSO senior managers may be held accountable by politicians for the overall achievements of their organisation, or for particular projects that have been implemented.

— *Financial accountability*: to those institutions that provide the financing for the organisation. For example, project managers may be held accountable by a funding organisation for the expenditure on their project.

— *Public accountability*: to citizens outside the organisation. For example, a Minister or Permanent Secretary may be held accountable by the public for corrupt activities within their Ministry. This is a combination of:

— ultimate political accountability, since public institutions are supposed to derive ultimate legitimacy from the citizenry, and

— client accountability, since citizens are normally the intended recipients of the services a PSO provides.

Other accountabilities include the *professional accountability* of staff to their professional peer group (e.g. social workers to other social workers); and *legal accountability* to the judiciary.

Within public sector organisations, accountability is often that of the individual for decisions made. Where accountability runs *outside* the organisation to other recipients, accountability is often aggregated to the level of the whole organisation. In other words, the whole organisation is somehow seen as accountable for the actions of its staff. Even in this case, individual senior staff may be held accountable by the external recipients. Those senior staff, in turn, may hold more junior individuals responsible within the organisation for externally-reported decisions and outcomes.

Accountability Outcomes Associated with New Computerised Information Systems

To what extent can the use of new computerised information systems support these various accountabilities? Evidence is drawn here from a number of cases, from which emerge four principal accountability impacts associated with information systems, particularly computerised information systems:

— essential support for accountability

— support for less than accountability

— alteration of the balance of accountabilities, and

— undermining of accountability.

These will now be investigated in turn. In each case, an attempt will be made to disentangle the broader role of information systems and the narrower role of information technology.

The creation of new information systems is an essential component in the creation of accountability. When a decision is taken, information about that decision and its outcomes must flow to all those to whom the decision maker is accountable. Without such an information flow and without the information system to carry that flow, there can be no accountability because there can be no knowledge of the decision.

"Essential to effective accountability for results (as well as good management) is credible, timely and relevant information on the performance of services and programs."

Accountability information systems are basically management information systems. They provide for the monitoring of decision performance, and are intended to assist in the control of that performance. As well as enabling new accountabilities, they can also improve existing ones through provision of more timely, consistent and formal information about performance.

In some cases, use of information technology forms an almost essential element of these new information systems. In one Asian railways information system, for instance, computerisation provided automated monitoring and comparison functions that would have been very hard to achieve using a non-computerised system.

However, computers are by no means always needed. One system of bringing local government officials in India to account used paper copies of financial statements pasted up in a public place, with no computers involved.

Those information systems with just a monitoring mechanism merely support *reporting*: recipients have information on decisions and outcomes but cannot judge them. Those with monitoring and comparison mechanisms merely support *openness*: recipients can judge whether decisions and outcomes meet acceptable performance standards but can do nothing with this information. Only those information systems that provide monitoring, comparison *and* control mechanisms can be said to truly support *accountability*: allowing recipients to take actions that affect the source decision maker.

For example, in India, a new (paper-based) public information system was created with the intention of improving accountability on rural development projects .

However, it only supported openness: citizens were able to monitor reported expenditure on local projects and compare it with actual project outcomes, thus identifying discrepancies in which public servants had embezzled funds. What the system did not do is provide a mechanism for actually holding decision makers accountable.

Information technology has tended to be used mainly to help create reporting or, to a lesser extent, openness information systems. It is rarely possible for IT to be applied in a full accountability system that automates control.

New information systems can expand the scope of accountability by delivering accountability information to new recipients. However, the effect in practice has been uneven. Those groups or institutions with the financial and political power to impose new information systems on public sector organisations are those to whom greater accountability has accrued.

This result has been seen particularly in the case of new information systems that are information technology-based and of powerful groups that are external to the PSO, such as:

— *Central government*. As central governments seek to enact reform measures, they seek greater control over, and accountability of, other parts of government. They have often used new computerised information systems in this effort. In Brazil, for example, the Ministry of Economics and Finance introduced a centralised, computerised financial administration information syste. This reported, and sanctioned payment for, the financial transactions of most government agencies. The effect was to increase the accountability of those agencies to central government.

— *Donors*. Funding agencies have been particularly active in formalising accountability relationships through the introduction of new computerised information systems:

"Many donors now increasingly look for mechanisms for effective project management, particularly financial management to be available. This is seen as providing the necessary feedback and control information to ensure managerial accountability over project implementation. ... That donors require this type of information from projects has led to their undertaking a programme of micro[*computer*] introduction to facilitate it."

Evidence indicates that such computerised systems will tend to drive out other information systems and channels. This occurs for a number of reasons:

— *Attention*: human attention capacity is limited. Where a recipient attends to formal computing information, s/he must necessarily remove attention from other information systems and channels. (This applies to any type of information system, IT-based or not, and means that some of the shifts described below can occur with or without computerisation.)

— *Information channel speed*: recipients select information channels mainly on the basis of speed and convenience rather than quality of information. Once installed, IT-based accountability systems will have a tendency to be relied on more and more because of this, again driving out other information systems and channels.

— *Personal preference*: some recipients prefer to receive information from inanimate objects. They will tend to focus increasingly on computerised information systems to the exclusion of other sources.

— *The mask of objectivity and data quality*. Insofar as computer-mediated communication channels are given greater (and often undue) credibility than other channels, the former will tend to drive out the latter. This issue is discussed again below.

The result is often a shift in the balance of information flows and accountability *from* citizens *to* central government and/or donors. This, in turn, leads PSOs to become more responsive to the demands of central government and/or donors, and less responsive to the needs of client groups.

There may also be a shift in focus from internal management to external groups. This has long been a problem with the external reporting of information in the public sector: that it consumes a large amount of internal resource, yet tends to undermine internal information systems and internal management processe. Internal information needs may be forgotten or, at best, be satisfied only where they overlap with the provisions of these external information systems.

This overlap between external information provision and internal information needs may be limited. Public sector systems for external reporting of accounts, for example, generally have to adhere to specified strict accounting principles, many of which are not relevant to internal needs. More than this, as noted below, there are frequent pressures to falsify externally-reported information.

Some public sector organisations have been driven to maintain two separate information systems: one for external consumption, and the real figures for internal use. Examples have been presented to the author from the public sector in one East African and one South Asian nation. In the former case, senior civil servants used one set of information for their own management purposes. A different set of information - mainly personnel and financial - was used to provide donors with a 'rosier-than-reality' picture of the progress of public sector reform.

In other cases, the situation might be reversed. The imposition of information systems may derive internally where, for example, a powerful senior manager pushes through their introduction. Again, there is likely be a growing imbalance of accountability in these situations, in this case away from external groups and institutions towards internal senior management.

Three scenarios have therefore been described that result from the introduction of new information systems, each of which leads to a shift in accountabilities:

— between external groups

— from internal management to particular external groups

— from external groups to internal management.

In all three cases, there is a process of polarisation in which the public at large - as both citizens and clients - are the 'accountability losers'.

As noted, these shifts can take place without the introduction of information technology. However, many of the new information systems are computer-based, and computerisation seems to give a boost to the imbalances of accountability that develop. This is ironic since much has been made of the potential for IT to create a greater direct accountability of PSOs to the public. There are, for instance, systems that provide public sector information via the Internet in many countries. Yet the information provided in such systems often consists of details about how to apply for public services; regulations governing business; and rose-tinted press releases ('cyberganda'). The presence of all this information helps divert attention from the fact that only rarely do such systems provide the type of information that allows public servants to be held to account.

Where accountability information *is* provided online, it can still reinforce inequities of accountability because of the accessibility barriers that computerised information systems raise (Cottrill 1995, Stoll 1995). Recipients must have access to the technology, and must have the skills and confidence to access and interpret the information provided. Central government and donor organisations have the resources to ensure they can overcome these barriers. This is the case for only a minority of public citizens in all countries.

When accountability information is available on paper, accessibility barriers are lower. Even here, some barriers remain, for recipients must generally be word-literate and statistically-literate to read and interpret the output. Citizens are still likely to be at a greater disadvantage than central government or donor organisations, though the 'disadvantage gap' should be less than with computerised systems.

This imbalance against the public is unlikely to be redressed unless the mass media plays a role. This role must be that of receiving, interpreting and publicising accountability information, and then of pressurising public officials on behalf of citizens.

From the previous sub-section, we may conclude that information systems in general can skew the balance of public sector accountabilities. *Computerised* information systems seem especially likely to contribute to this skew. Continuing the specific focus on information technology, potential impacts are discussed below which may sometimes undermine the whole process of accountability.

Computerisation may be associated with a loss of paper records, and this can have a significant impact on accountability. As Cain points out, computerised records currently provide a far poorer basis for accountability than paper-based records because of their intangibility and malleability. Unless there is a concerted and continuing effort to maintain paper records, accountability can be undermined with the advent of computerisation.

The mask of data quality

Where they know they are being judged by others on the basis of the data provided, sources will tend to provide inaccurate data. The expectation is therefore that large amounts of the information provided by accountability information systems cannot be relied upon.

The problem with computerisation is that the introduction of IT *per se* has little effect on data quality.

Worse, the - often inaccurate - data within computerised accountability systems is given credibility because of the perceived objectivity of computers. Computerisation can lead recipients to believe in inaccurate accountability information, thus undermining the process of accountability.

Even if the data is accurate, there may be problems because of the way in which computerised systems tend to drive out other information channels. Where accountability IS are computer-based, recipients may increasingly take the accountability IS data at face value and may base accountability decisions on it alone. Where recipients ignore other information channels and fail to cross-check via informal consultations, the validity of the accountability process is likely to suffer.

In an African public works department, computerisation of the payroll system allowed a computer operator to enter the details of 'ghost workers', whose wages he was able to collect. Computerisation undermined accountability in this case by opening access to corruption opportunities for computing staff, whilst reducing the ability of non IT-literate managers to monitor and control the payroll system.

Separate from the issue of the accountability information systems themselves is a problem raised by the introduction of other computerised information systems into public sector organisations. Such systems automate human labour and thus reduce human inputs to the decision-making process, sometimes to the extent of removing them altogether.

This leads to a confusion and undermining of accountability, because it produces the question: "Who is to be held accountable when computerised information systems are involved in decisions and subsequent actions that are judged to be sub-standard?". This question keeps thousands of lawyers busy worldwide in liability lawsuits.

Although one might look forward to the day when PCs are locked up in jail for their misdemeanours, information technology cannot be held accountable for its actions. Mistakes are frequently and conveniently blamed on 'computer errors' or 'software bugs' but, in law and in current reality, this is not reasonable. Such mistakes can almost always be traced back to a human root.

The problem for accountability, to the delight of the lawyers, is the difficulty of which human root to trace it back to. A faulty decision outcome arising from use of a typical management support system (MSS) could derive from many sources, including:

— MSS development problems, such as poor analysis or poor specification or poor design of the system

— MSS implementation problems, such as the introduction of a software bug or inadequate training

— sub-standard manufacture of the MSS hardware, such as the installation of a faulty chip

— MSS operational problems, such as mistyping or poor maintenance or virus infection

— MSS use problems, such as human error by the manager making use of the system output.

Each source in itself can be many-layered. For example, if the software system has a bug that leads to damaging decisions, who is to be held accountable: the programmer who put in the bug; the system tester who failed to spot it; the system designer who chose that particular programming language and complex software design; the project manager overseeing the whole process; the PSO manager who commissioned the system; etc.?

The use of *computerised* information systems in decision making can therefore cloud more than clarify accountability.

Factors Determining accountability outcomes

Information systems can support or alter or undermine accountability. How can we explain this variety of different impacts? The first step is to understand both information technology and information systems as part of a broader context. Drawing from innumerable other works on information systems, a summary framework of IT and IS context is presented.

Each one of this diagram's factors, alone or in combination, can be seen to have an effect on accountability outcomes. Here, the factors will be discussed under four headings.

Information Technology

Information technology generally provides a reporting of information that transmits information from the source decision maker to the recipient. At best, it can provide an openness that compares this information to pre-set norms and alerts recipients when there is some deviation. It cannot create complete accountability because it has no innate accountability property. Thus, IT is not always essential in accountability information systems. Indeed, as described above, IT seems to skew or undermine accountability more easily than increasing it.

Wider Systems Design : If information technology alone cannot create accountability, then simultaneously-introduced, wider systems components are required if accountability is to be achieved. These components - people, management and processes - are part of the overall information system, but they are also related to wider organisational systems components such as strategies and structures. They must exist around both the accountability source and the recipient:

Source factors

— *People*: Over and above most other factors, there must be a motivation of public servants to act accountably. This, in turn, depends on many other factors such as current rewards within the job for performing well; the likelihood of detection and punishment for wrong-doing; and the organisational culture's viewpoint on accountability.

— *Management*: Within public sector organisations, there must be a system of managerial responsibility that informs decision makers of their responsibilities and identifies those who are responsible. One common fudge in accountability information systems is the identification of a shortcoming but a failure to identify who specifically is responsible for that shortcoming. This is corporate accountability without individual accountability.

If the accountability information system is to move beyond just reporting, some type of performance standard must be set. Reported information can then be compared against this standard to determine what is and is not satisfactory. Both source and recipient should be aware of these measures.

— *Processes*: The processes must exist to gather accountability information and deliver it to relevant recipients.

Recipient factors

— *People*: Those wishing to hold public servants accountable must have the skills to access information systems and interpret results. They must also be motivated to hold public servants accountable. This last point cannot always be assumed: some public information systems in the West are marked less by the enthusiasm of a minority of citizens than by the apathy and disinterest of the majority.

— *Management*: Those wishing to hold public servants accountable must have the authority to demand explanations from public servants, and to affect those public servants with their subsequent actions. Appropriate structures must therefore be in place to permit this. Taking a UK example, one of the aims of the Citizen's Charter - besides publicising information about performance - has been to create an easy-to-use complaints and feedback system.

— *Processes*: Comparison and control processes must exist that allow recipients to interpret accountability information in the light of performance standards; to communicate with public servants in order to supplement the formal accountability information with informal contextual information; and then to decide upon and implement appropriate control actions.

Returning to an earlier example, the rural poor in the state of Rajasthan in India undertook an accountability action. Here, the people components were definitely in place as regards the recipients, who had a deep desire to hold public servants accountable for money that was being corruptly diverted from development projects. However, the management authority, structures and processes to then call the public servants to account and affect them with actions were not present. This is therefore a case of openness without accountability: new information flows made citizens aware of wrong-doing by public servants, but they had little ability to interact with the public servants and little power to correct those wrong-doings.

The Process of Information System Design

The method of design strongly shapes the design and operation of the information system it produces. The designers of an accountability information systems must therefore themselves be accountable to the intended recipients of accountability information.

In some cases, this is so. Where central government or donor organisations introduce an accountability information system, for example, they often fund it and 'call the shots' as far as system design is concerned.

The same is less likely to be true of managerial or public accountability systems. Here, the systems designers may have little meaningful interaction with the intended recipients. Instead, they design the information system to the requirements they believe the recipients have, or to the requirements of the source decision makers. In either case, the resulting information system may not support accountability.

Organisational and Environmental Factors

Given the flexibility of information technology and information systems, accountability impacts are strongly determined by the management decisions of those creating the accountability information systems. In turn, these decisions will themselves be affected by a range of wider factors.

Taking the Indian case once again, accountability information systems were largely shaped by an organisational politics of self-interest and a culture of corruption prior to the actions of a non-government organisation (the MKSS: Mazdoor Kisan Shakti Sangathan) in pressurising government for more access to information. In theory, before the MKSS' actions, there were accountability systems passing information up to higher levels within the public sector organisations involved and to external, central government institutions. In practice, the politics and culture ensured there was no accountability because the information transmitted was largely false and because higher levels were not motivated to try to hold development staff accountable.

The actions of institutions in this case - the MKSS on behalf of the rural poor of Rajasthan and, probably much more importantly, the mass media that picked up the story and publicised it - changed the external environment, and led to changes at the level of the state government. However, this did little to effect the ongoing politics and culture. Overall, then, negligible progress was actually made in holding public servants accountable.

Clearly computerisation is no panacea for achieving accountability. Information technology has no innate impact on accountability and, whilst it may support some accountability information systems, it is not typically essential. Where present, computers may skew or undermine accountability as much as support it.

Information technology may not be essential to accountability, but the same is not true of information and information systems. Information flows (hence, information systems) enable accountability and are essential to it. Nevertheless, like IT, information systems are flexible and have no pre-determined impact on accountability.

In some cases, new information systems have been associated with positive accountability outcomes for certain stakeholders. In other cases, though, even when a working information system is produced, there may be components of IS failure, such as:

— *goals unattained for particular stakeholders*: this will occur, for example, if the new IS only assists reporting rather than accountability, or if the new IS undermines accountability by giving credibility to inaccurate data

— *undesirable outcomes for particular stakeholders*: this will occur, for example, if the introduction of a donor-oriented IS leads to a reduction in accountability to the public.

In all, we may conclude that information systems, particularly their technology component, have had only a limited positive impact on accountability initiatives in the public sector.

Information systems *per se* do not cause or even significantly drive accountability. Instead, the key to accountability outcomes lies within the shell of surrounding factors illustrated in figure 3. Within this shell, it is management decisions about the information systems and their design processes that are fundamental. These decisions, in turn, are affected by factors such as organisational politics and culture, and the external environment.

Thus, not surprisingly, accountability outcomes associated with IT are not equal across all types of accountability but have tended to follow existing distributions of power. As a generalisation, computerised accountability IS initiatives in the public sector appear to have supported:

— financial accountability to some extent

— managerial accountability to a limited extent

— political accountability to a very limited extent, and

— public accountability hardly at all.

This hierarchy typically reflects the hierarchy of political will and power identified in section 1.

Achieving Accountability

For any type of accountability to be achieved, there must a fit between all the factors identified.

— the process of information systems design

— the technology; the skills and processes of the information system

— personal motivations of the stakeholders

— management strategies and values

— organisational structures, politics and culture.

In certain public sector situations - currently characterised by limited accountability and even corruption - this fit will be hard to achieve because it requires such a combination of changes. This includes changes not just in the information systems architecture but also, quite probably, in the way that information systems are designed and implemented. In addition, there will be the wider linked changes that are required in organisational political and bureaucratic structures, strategies, culture and so on.

Within each of these changes, there will be inertia at work that will tend to reinforce the status quo, such as:

— a *technological inertia* because of the high financial and skills costs of introducing IT or of changing the current computing architecture

— a *management inertia* because managers are used to making work decisions, including those on information systems, in a particular way

— a *political inertia* because those involved will not wish to give up their information and power by becoming more accountable.

It is possible to overcome such inertia, but only where change is driven from an environmental and organisational level. In other words, referring back to figure 3, change will be driven from the outer shells inward far more easily than it can be driven from the inner shells outward.

In practice, this means that successful accountability initiatives will require consensus amongst the key stakeholders about the desirability of accountability. Such consensus may derive from factors within the organisation (such as self-interest, and reward and punishment systems) or from outside the organisation (such as pressure from politicians, international organisations, or the public via the mass media). Where such consensus is absent, the risk of failure is high for any accountability IS project.

Implications for Information Systems Design

The role of the IS design method in determining accountability outcomes has been described above. In this final section, though, the focus will be on stakeholder perceptions of likely accountability outcomes, and the impact of those perceptions on IS design.

Although the impact may be limited in practice, public servants often perceive that new information systems - especially computerised information systems - *are* going to have a have significant effect of increasing accountability (and, hence, reducing corruption). These perceptions will feed into the process of planning any new information system. The effect of these perceptions is likely to be particularly marked where a new computer system is being introduced in the presence of practices that are currently unaccountable.

For instance, in one Asian government's pensions office, studied by the author, computerisation was roundly resisted. Many factors were at first seen to underlie the resistance including:

— fears of loss of jobs

— fears that staff would not have the necessary skills

— health and safety concerns.

What emerged during investigation, however, was that the main fear lay around the issue of corrupt incomes. Pensions staff had the power to deny claimants access to pension payments or to provide claimants with access to certain types of higher-income pension. The staff were using this power to extract bribes from pensionable claimants. They feared that computerisation would create accountability in the pension payment process and would therefore remove this power. Hence, their true reason for resistance.

Where resistance and lack of accountability are linked, there are three possible reactions:

— if the new information system will not have an effect, make this (subtly) clear

— if the new information system will increase accountability and the stakeholders are not that powerful, then 'tough it out', i.e. push on in the likelihood that resistance can be overcome

— if the new information system will increase accountability and the stakeholders are powerful, change the IS design plans so that the key unaccountable processes are not computerised or are not exposed to monitoring by the computerised information system.

'Toughing it out' can also be tried in the last case, and this would seem to be the morally-correct route to take. However, it will greatly increase resistance to the new information system and the risks of IS failure.

Whatever the reaction, it is clear that the link between new information systems and accountability will have to be recognised in the planning of some information systems. This link must also be teased out as a component of resistance to computerisation.

4

Internet Service Providers

The Internet industry continues to expand in China, the government continues to tighten controls on on-line expression. As recently as July 11, 2001, President Jiang Zemin condemned the spread of "pernicious information" on the Net and called existing legislation "inadequate." Since 1995, when Chinese authorities began permitting commercial Internet accounts, at least sixty sets of regulations have been issued aimed at controlling Internet content. The broadly-worded regulations represent a clear violation of the right to freedom of expression, and the government is devoting considerable time and resources to trying to implement them.

As of January 2001, sending "secret" or "reactionary" materials over the Internet became a capital crime. Generally, however, persons convicted for their use of the Internet have received sentences of between two and four years, and we are not aware of anyone having been charged under Internet-specific regulations. Instead, they have all been found guilty of violating provisions of the Criminal Code. The elaborate regulatory framework serves, however, as a statement of policy, a justification for monitoring and surveillance, a set of guidelines for what constitutes "illegal" activity, and a deterrent to Internet users.

The government's determination to censor on-line content has grown with Internet usage. Improved infrastructure, introduction of mobile phones, and other low-cost methods of connection to the Internet, as well as increased local language content, have fueled that growth. The main contact points connecting China's Internet system with the worldwide system consists of nine so-called Internet Access Providers controlling the physical lines to the outside world. By July 2001 these access providers accommodated some 620 Internet Service Providers (ISPs) who served in turn some 1,600 Internet Content Providers (ICPs) and an estimated 26,000,000 users by the government's own conservative estimates.

This backgrounder examines the development of China's repressive regulatory framework, its surveillance and closures of Internet cafés, and the detention of Internet users.

Between 1994 and the present, China's rules and regulations on the Internet became progressively more comprehensive, moving from efforts to regulate Internet business to restrictions on news sites and chat rooms. These regulations give the government wide discretion to arrest and punish any form of expression. For example, "topics that damage the reputation of the State" are banned, but an Internet user has no way of knowing what topics might be considered injurious. As the regulatory framework evolved, the Chinese government shifted primary responsibility for control of the Internet from the Ministry for Public Security to the Internet service providers themselves.

In 1994, one year before the Internet became commercially available for individuals in China, the State Council issued the "PRC Regulations for the Safety Protection of Computer Information Systems" which gave the Ministry of Public Security overall responsibility for supervision of the Internet. According to the regulations, Public Security is entitled to "supervise, inspect and guide the security protection work," "investigate and prosecute illegal criminal cases" and "perform other supervising duties." In February 1996, the State Council issued rules on the connection between China's domestic network and the international Internet. These regulations began to shift some of the responsibility for control of content to the Internet companies themselves.

Units providing international inward and outward channels and interactive and interfacing units shall establish a network management center to strengthen the management of their own units and their consumers according to the relevant laws and state regulation, to improve network information security management, and to provide good and safe services to consumers.

Units and individuals engaging in Internet business shall strictly enforce safety and security control systems according to relevant state laws and administrative regulations, and shall not make use of the Internet to conduct criminal activities - including activities prejudicial to state security and the leakage of state secrets - or to produce, retrieve, duplicate, and disseminate information prejudicial to public order or pornographic materials."

Public Security then issued a decree that all Internet users register with a police bureau in their neighborhood within thirty days of signing up with an ISP. Police stations in provinces and cities followed up on this almost immediately. They also set up computer investigation units. In December 1997, the "Computer Information Network and Internet Security, Protection and Management Regulations," issued by the Ministry of Public Security, states:

No unit or individual may use the Internet to create, replicate, retrieve, or transmit the following kinds of information:

1. Inciting to resist or violate the Constitution or laws or the implementation of administrative regulations;
2. Inciting to overthrow the government or the socialist system;
3. Inciting division of the country, harming national unification;
4. Inciting hatred or discrimination among nationalities or harming the unity of the nationalities;
5. Making falsehoods or distorting the truth, spreading rumors, destroying the order of society;
6. Promoting feudal superstitions, sexually suggestive material, gambling, violence, murder,
7. Engaging in terrorism or inciting others to criminal activity; openly insulting other people or distorting the truth to slander people;
8. Injuring the reputation of state organs;

Other activities against the Constitution, laws or administrative regulations.

Units and individuals engaged in Internet business must accept the security supervision, inspection, and guidance of the Public Security organization. This includes providing to the Public Security organization information, materials and digital document, and assisting the Public Security organization to discover and properly handle incidents involving law violations and criminal activities related to computer information networks.

The main two sets of regulations that foreign investors such as AOL will have to confront are the "Telecommunications Regulations Of The People's Republic Of China" and the "Measures For Managing The Internet Information Services," both issued by the State Council and effective from September 25, 2000.

The Telecommunications Regulations state that:

No organization or individual may use telecommunications networks to make, duplicate, issue, or disseminate information containing the following:

1) Material that opposes the basic principles established by the constitution;
2) Material that jeopardizes national security, reveals state secrets, subverts state power, or undermines national unity;
3) Material that harms the prosperity and interests of the state;
4) Material that arouses ethnic animosities, ethnic discrimination, or undermines ethnic solidarity;
5) Material that undermines state religious policies, or promotes cults and feudal superstitions;

6) Material that spreads rumors, disturbs social order, or undermines social stability;
7) Material that spreads obscenities, pornography, gambling, violence, murder, terror, or instigates crime;
8) Material that insults or slanders others or violates the legal rights and interests of others;
9) Material that has other contents prohibited by laws or administrative regulations.

Meanwhile the "Measures For Managing The Internet Information Services" make service providers responsible for content they display. The service providers must record their subscribers' access to the Internet, their account numbers, the Web addresses they call up as well as the telephone numbers they use, and store this information for sixty days. The eight categories of information that is not to be produced on the Internet. Article 16 then goes on saying that if material under these categories is discovered, "it shall immediately stop the transmission, keep the relevant records, and report the situation to the relevant state authorities."

Other regulations that content providers have to face include the "State Secrets Protection Regulations For Computer Information Systems On The Internet" issued by the Bureau for the Protection of State Secrets (State Secrets Bureau) on January 25, but applied retroactively from January 1, 2000.

The management of secrets concerning information on the Internet shall be based on the principle of "whoever places materials on the Internet takes the responsibility." Information provided to or released on

Web sites must undergo a security inspection and approval. Inspection and approval should be carried out by related departments. Related units shall, in line with state laws and regulations on guarding secrets, establish and improve a leadership responsibility system for the examination and approval of information intended for the Internet. Units that provide the information shall establish a security system for information examination and approval in accordance with certain work procedures.

Units and users that establish electronic bulletin boards, chat rooms or network news groups shall be verified and approved by the relevant organizations to clarify the requirements and responsibilities concerning the protection of secrets. No unit or individual shall release, discuss or disseminate information about state secrets on electronic bulletin boards, chat rooms or network news groups.

For electronic bulletin boards, chat rooms or network news groups that are open to the public, the host or its higher level competent department shall strictly carry out its responsibilities concerning the protection of secrets, establish a complete management system, and strengthen supervision and inspection. If information related to secrets is discovered, it shall take timely measures and report this to the local authorities for the protection of secrets.

The regulations demand that Internet Access Providers:

> Shall provide instruction about protecting secrets as an important part of the Internet related technical training. Agreements and user rules signed between the controllers of national trunk lines and Internet

> access providers, and between Internet access providers and users shall stipulate clearly that state laws on protecting secrets must be obeyed and that state secrets shall not be leaked.

Article 15 states:

Controllers of national trunk lines, Internet access providers and users shall accept the supervision and inspection conducted by departments in charge of protecting secrets and shall cooperate with them. They shall assist such departments in investigating illegal actions that divulge state secrets on the Internet. They shall also delete information on the Internet that concerns state secrets, as required by the departments in charge of protecting secrets.

Violation of the regulations mentioned above can lead to severe punishment. Content and service providers may face fines or closure, but users found in violation may face the death penalty for posting material that is not to the government's liking. On December 2000, the "Decisions Of The National People's Congress Standing Committee On Safeguarding Internet Safety" stipulated that:

> in order to maintain national security and social stability, one who commits any of the following acts, which constitute a crime, will be prosecuted for criminal liability in accordance with relevant regulations of the criminal law.

1) Fabricating rumors or slander, or publishing or disseminating other harmful information through the Internet to instigate subversion of state power, overthrow the socialist system, or incite the splitting of the country to damage national reunification;

2) Stealing or disclosing state secrets, information or military secrets through the Internet;

3) Instigating national hostility and discrimination through the Internet to damage national unity;

Organizing evil cults and contacting cult members through the Internet to damage the implementation of state law and administrative laws and regulations.

In January 2001, possibly as a result of the imminent publication of the Tiananmen Papers, the collection of documents about decision-making by senior Chinese officials with regard to the student protests of 1989, the Supreme People's Court set the ultimate punishment:

Those who illegally provide state secrets or intelligence for units, organizations and individuals outside the country through Internet with serious consequences will be punished according to stipulations of the Criminal Law.... in especially serious cases, those who steal, make secret inquiries or buy state secrets and intelligence and illegally provide gathered state secrets and intelligence to units outside the country will be sentenced to ten or more years of fixed-term imprisonment or imprisonment for life and their properties may concurrently be confiscated by the state. In cases of a gross violation of law and where especially serious harm is caused to the state and people, law offenders may be sentenced to death and their properties will be confiscated by the state.

Internet Cafes

In practice the regulations have led Internet service and content providers and Internet cafés to set up their own monitors. In organizations like Sohu.com, a Nasdaq registered portal based in Beijing, appointed censors are monitoring the chatrooms and the bulletin boards and deleting material mentioned under the eight categories under the September 2000 "Measures For Managing The Internet Information Services." In Internet cafes, managers have appointed people who patrol the monitors checking what material appears on the screen. Both Internet content providers such as Sohu.com and Internet Cafes have issued their own sets of guidelines for users. Sohu.com, for example, gives the following message to clients who want to enter chatrooms: Please take note that the following issues are prohibited according to Chinese law:

1. Criticism of the PRC Constitution
2. Revealing State secrets, and discussion about overthrowing the Communist government
3. Topics that damage the reputation of the State
4. Discussions that ignite ethnic animosity, discrimination or regional separatism
5. Discussion that undermines the state's religious policy, as well as promotes evil cults and superstition
6. Spreading rumors, perpetrating and disseminating false news that promotes disorder and social instability
7. Dissemination of obscenity, sex, gambling, violence, and terror. Cyber-sex is not permitted within the English chat-room.
8. Humiliating or slandering innocent people

9. Any discussion and promotion of content which PRC laws prohibit.

If you are a Chinese national and willingly choose to break these laws, Sohu.com is legally obliged to report you to the Public Security Bureau.

Personnel of the Beijing-based Feiyu Internet Cafe routinely check screens by walking along the 800 computer units and reading over the shoulders of the clients. A note which is placed on a user's monitor to indicate the start of his or her login time, says "The Feiyu Web Bar Warns its Clients: Please do Not Download Web Pages with Illicit, Violent or Reactionary Content..." Content considered "reactionary" can include Falun Gong-related material, dissident web pages or sites promoting the independence of Taiwan or Tibet. Feiyu's website has a link to all major Internet regulations and added some additional ones. Under these rules, mostly issued by the Bureau of Industry and Commerce, Feiyu management is obliged to turn violators in to the local police station. In December, the China Daily reported that police raided the Feiyu Cafe and found some "illegal content," but the management was only fined, and business was back to normal after some hours.

On April 10, 2001, the State Council announced a three-month investigation into Internet cafés and other public Internet service providers. A conference, jointly held by the Ministry of Information Industry, the Ministry of Public Security, the Ministry of Culture and the State Administration of Industry and Commerce, then issued an order saying that within this period, no new Internet cafés would be approved. The moratorium was accompanied by an extensive checking of existing cafés nationwide during which the latter were obliged to re-

register. The Legal Daily gave what it termed an "incomplete" progress report on June 14, 2001. By that time, police had investigated more than 56,800 "web bars," of which 6,071 were ordered to disconnect from the Internet. Between April and July 2001, over 2,300 cafés had been closed down altogether. Special measures were taken in some provinces. Police in Liaoning province installed software in 13,500 computers in the province's 5,000 Internet cafes to automatically filter pornographic, illicit and other harmful information. The raids were carried out "in order to rectify and standardize the order of the market economy" according to the paper.

Several individuals have been detained as a result of posting material on the Internet. In all known cases they were sentenced under articles in the Criminal Code.

Qi Yanchen is one of the founders of the China Development Union, a quasi-nongovernmental organization which was banned in late 1998. Qi was detained in late 1999. In September 2000, the Intermediate People's Court in Cangzhou, Hebei Province sentenced him to four years in prison for posting articles and parts of his book, The Collapse of China, on the Internet. The book is critical of China's current social situation. Qi was charged with spreading anti-government messages on the Internet and was convicted after a trial that lasted four and a half hours.

Huang Qi, a computer engineer, was charged with the crime of "instigation to subvert state power." Huang, together with his wife Zeng Li, ran www.6-4tianwang.com, a website designed to find missing persons. On June 3, 2000, authorities in Chengdu, Sichuan province, detained Huang after they deemed the content posted "subversive." On September 25, Huang Qi was reportedly beaten in detention by three policemen after notes he had taken were confiscated. During the beating, he lost one tooth and got a scar on his forehead, according to a letter he gave to his lawyer in November. On January 2, 2001, the Chengdu City Procuratorate accused Huang Qi of violating Articles 103 and 105 of the Criminal Law. The articles punish actions that involve "organizing national separatism, destroying national unity"; "organizing, plotting or carrying out activities aimed at subverting state political power"; and "overthrowing the socialist system." Huang's trial began on February 13, 2001, but the trial was suspended indefinitely after he reportedly fell ill. It was re-scheduled for June 27, but again postponed. No reason for the delay was announced, nor was a new trial date scheduled.

Jiang was a teacher with the No. 9 Middle School in Nanchong, Sichuan province and owner of the Silicon Valley Internet Cafe in Nanchong. He was detained on August 16, 2000, five days after posting a series of articles critical of the Chinese government on an Internet bulletin board. He was charged with "subverting state political power." The Nanchong Intermediate People's Court sentenced him to two years in prison. In May 2001, a higher court in Sichuan rejected his appeal.

Guo Qinghai, a freelance writer, was arrested on September 15, 2000. On April 3, a court in Cangzhou, Hebei province tried and sentenced him to four years in prison. Guo was charged with "inciting to overthrow state political power." Guo had posted some forty articles on the Internet and published in the Hong Kong based magazine Kaifang calling for political reform. No one informed the family before the two-hour trial began, and as a result no family member attended. Guo did not have a lawyer for his defense.

Lu Xinhua, the author of several articles published on overseas websites, was detained on March 11, 2001 for "subversion." According to the Information Center for Human Rights and Democracy, Lu was formally arrested on April 20.

Yang Zili, a Beijing based computer engineer, is the founder of the Internet site www.lib.126.com. He was detained on March 13, 2001. Authorities have not given an explanation for his detention as yet. Yang had criticized the crackdown against the Falun Gong on his website. He also used the site to teach people how to use proxy servers, a way to circumvent censorship and access sites blocked by the Ministry of Information Industry.

Xu, a reporter and a founding member of the "New Youth Study Group," was detained in Beijing on March 13, 2001 for subversion. He was reportedly targeted for his use of the Internet and his association with the study group, which focuses on political reforms.

Jin, a geological engineer and a founding member of the "New Youth Study Group," was detained in Beijing on March 13, 2001 for subversion. He was reportedly targeted for his use of the Internet and his association with the study group, which focuses on political reforms.

Zhang, a freelance writer and a founding member of the "New Youth Study Group," was detained in Beijing on March 13, 2001 for subversion. He was reportedly targeted for his use of the Internet and his association with the study group, which focuses on political reforms

On April 18, 2001, police detained Chi, a worker in Changchun, Jilin province. They found on him articles with political content which he had downloaded from overseas websites. As of April 2001, he was detained in Lingyuan Prison, Liaoning Province.

Wang was taken into custody on May 6, 2001 from his home in Lingyi, Shandong for "libeling police on the Internet" but it is not clear what the content was of his allegedly libelous remarks.

Hu Dalin was detained on May 18, 2001, apparently for helping his father, a leftwing essayist named Lu Jiaping, post his writings on websites. The authorities were particularly angry over an article by the father about the case of the U.S. spy plane forced to land in China. The article was posted on May 11, 2001.

In June 2001, authorities in Xinjiang Autonomous Region sentenced Liu Weifang, a small business owner, to three years in prison for posting "reactionary articles" criticizing the Chinese Communist Party and its leaders on Internet bulletin boards. He had used his Internet name, lgwf, but authorities traced the messages to him. The Xinjiang Daily said Liu got off lightly because he had admitted guilt.

Wang, a former assistant professor of psychology at Southwestern Normal University in Chongqing, Sichuan, was arrested on June 2, 2001 in Shenzhen for downloading and distributing by e-mail promotional material on the Falungong spiritual movement.

Li, a businessman from central Hunan, was reportedly detained after e-mailing the Chinese language version of The Tiananmen Papers to friends. He was detained in Shaoyang, Hunan, as of July 2001 according to the Hong Hong-based Information Center for Human Rights and Democracy.

1. Agence France Presse, "Jiang Renews Warning Against 'Pernicious' Internet," July 11, 2001.

2. Eight separate ministries or government agencies, led by the Ministry of Public Security, are involved in Internet monitoring and control. They include the Ministry of Information Industry, the Standing Committee of the National People's Congress, the State Council, the Supreme People's Court, the State Bureau for the Protection of Secrets, the State Administration for Press and Publications, and the State Copyright Bureau.

3. "China to Speed up Internet," People's Daily, July 11, 2001.

4. PRC Regulations for the Safety Protection of Computer Information Systems (Zhonghua renmin gongheguo jisuanji xitong anquan baohu tiaoli,) Fazhi Ribao (Legal Daily), February 24, 1994, issued by State Council Order No.147, signed by Premier Li Peng on February 18, 1994.

5. PRC Interim Regulations Governing the Management of International Computer Networks (Zhonghua renmin gongheguo jisuanji xinxi wangluo guoji lianwang guanli zanxing guiding), Fazhi Ribao (Legal Daily), February 12, 1996, issued by State Council Order No.195, signed by Premier Li Peng on February 1, 1996.

6. Management Measures of the PRC Regulations for the Safety Protection of Computer Information Systems (Jisuanji xinxi wangluo guoji lianwang anquan baohu guanli banfa.), in Jisuanji Ji Wangluo - Falu Fagui (Computers and Internet Laws and Regulations), Falu Chubanshe, Beijing: 1999, p. 99. These regulations were published in full by some Internet cafés. See also the website of Feiyu, an Internet café in Beijing.

7. PRC Telecommunications Regulations (Zhonghua renmin gongheguo dianxin tiaoli),.October 11, 2000, issued by State Council Order No.291, signed by Premier Zhu Rongji on September 25, 2000. Measures for Managing Internet Information Services (Hulianwang xinxi fuwu guanli banfa.), Fazhi Ribao (Legal Daily), issued by State Council Order No.292; signed by Premier Zhu Rongji on September 25, 2000.

8. Regulations Regarding Management of Secrets in Computer Information Systems and International Internet.

9. Decisions of the National People's Congress Standing Committee on Safeguarding Internet Safety.

10. Explanations on Certain Questions Concerning the Specific Application of Law in the Trial of Cases of Stealing, Making Secret Inquiries of or Buying State Secrets and Intelligence and Illegally Providing Gathered State Secrets and Intelligence for Units Outside the Country, in "China: Supreme People's Court on Stealing State Secrets, BBC Monitoring, January 23, 2001, from Xinhua, January 21, 2001.

5

Encryption

Strong encryption poses to public safety and national security; indeed, some of the more extreme rhetoric paints computer encryption as though it were the most dangerous technological innovation since the atom bomb. My intent in this presentation is to illuminate why strong encryption is critical to the human rights movement, and how considerations of privacy, free expression, and even protection of human life raise deep concerns regarding some proposed controls on encryption. Human Rights Watch has not evaluated the specific provisions of the various legislative proposals tabled, nor is it at this time putting forth a model policy on encryption. It is, however, committed to the belief that encryption is an extremely important bulwark against grave human rights abuses, and that United States policy on encryption will have global ramifications.

Encryption and the Human Rights Movement

It is important to keep in mind that there is nothing new about cryptography or the use of codes, as Peter Wayner reminded us in this Tuesday's *New York Times.* Those who have relied on coded speech include not merely spies and criminals, but patriots such as Thomas Jefferson, dissidents such as Andrei Sakharov, political prisoners such as Doan Viet Hoat, and human rights organizations such as Human Rights Watch or Amnesty International. What is new is the Internet, a medium that enables swift and inexpensive global communication between individuals from every point on earth, and which promises to destroy the ability of abusive regimes to silence their people, hide their atrocities, and blockade the truth.

There has been no time that human rights concerns have been more visible than recent years as networks of local and international activists bring abuses to light. Global integration of telephone and fax lines are a direct cause. Whereas before we would wait months to learn of the arrest and imprisonment of dissidents in Vietnam, today their relatives simply call human rights monitors and the United Nations—leading to the paradox that it is easier to report on human rights in that country from abroad than within. Before, the government could easily suppress the dissemination of critical essays and monographs; today, writers can transmit their writings outside the country for distribution via the Internet. In Bosnia, Chechnya and Congo human rights monitors relay minute-by-minute information via satellite. Our organization has been able to help human rights activists escape at the height of the genocide in Rwanda and the coup in Cambodia thanks to the medium of telephone and fax. It is not accidental that the rise in global communications has coincided with the strongest world efforts yet to end impunity for heinous abuses, in the establishment of international criminal tribunals, truth commissions, peacekeeping missions, and the like. Far from producing a jaded public, the exposure of these crimes to light has fed a demand for justice.

It is no surprise that abusive authorities see the Internet as a threat and have tried to censor and control it, to some effect. In Burma, the SLORC has made it illegal to own any personal computer with networking hardware unless authorized by the government. Iraq this year announced a total ban on Internet access. The United Arab Emirates grants Internet access licenses through the police, and a man has been arrested in Bahrain on suspicion of transmitting information about the internal situation to persons abroad via the Internet. Vietnam and China and monitor political content on the Internet and block access to sites. In South Korea, you can be prosecuted for trying to access a North Korean Web page, and should you meet a North Korean on the Internet you must report to the police within seven days.

Encryption offers the most fundamental protection to those who seek to bring abuses to light in these circumstances. Every activist can reel off situations where some victim of abuse could have been protected, some human rights monitor spared retaliation, or some perpetrator exposed, had secure communication been possible. The implications for international efforts to end impunity are enormous. Presently, international organizations, to say nothing of local groups, are hobbled in how much information they can safely archive or transmit in conflict situations without jeopardizing the lives of witnesses and victims. It was only the U.S. government, for example, that had the capability to transport the documentation of Iraq's genocidal Anfal campaign against the Kurds. Censorship, intimidation and disinformation may lose much of their force if secure avenues of communication are opened to individuals around the world.

Already, human rights groups in Hong Kong, anticipating greater controls on free expression, have planned mirror sites where there information may be available globally even if it is restricted in Hong Kong. In China, dissidents have established an anonymous electronic journal that they send to a site in the United States, from whence it is returned to Chinese e-mail addresses via a virtually untraceable distribution system. Encryption has the power to authenticate the identity of these authors to their partners abroad, and protect their identity from despots at home.

Encryption is also a means of authentication. Digital signatures are the encryption of message digests that can be decrypted by the recipient to verify both the identity of the sender and that the message has not subsequently been altered by anyone else. The value of this in commercial transactions is obvious, but it is also vital to human rights work. To be effective, human rights groups must build a reputation for responsible, accurate and unbiased reporting.

Once a group has a reputation, others may wish to capitalize on it by impersonating the group. Human Rights Watch frequently must disavow connection with other groups who seek to capitalize on the "Watch" name and reputation. More sinister is the attempt of groups or governments to deliberately issue false or misleading information in the name of a human rights group. Impersonation can also be used to gain the trust of sources and expose dissidents and informants to persecution.

To serve any of these functions, encryption must be effective. It must be strong, with key lengths that prevent easy decryption, it must be available worldwide, and keys to codes must be secure against those who would use them abusively to intercept messages or impersonate authors.

Why are these concerns relevant to United States domestic encryption policy? One reason is that the United States has traditionally been in the forefront of defining and protecting freedom of expression. Any regime adopted in this country will have profound influence on what other governments do and how they justify it. We will be in a poor position to criticize abusively implemented restrictions placed on electronic communications if they are patterned on our own. There are many countries even where court supervision of government communication intercepts would offer little or no protection, because courts are not independent.

Another reason is that it is inevitable that our government on occasion will wish to share decrypted information, either for purposes of law enforcement, diplomacy, or defense of national security. There is nothing particularly alarming about the sharing of legitimately-gathered intelligence or investigatory materials *per se,* but when those materials are obtained from using a private party's key, several concerns arise. One is the possibility that the key itself may be shared or communicated—thus opening the door to future surveillance of every conversation or file of the targeted individual. This is roughly analogous to not just giving a third party the transcript of a wiretap, but handing over the actual wiretap setup as well. Two, the acquisition by our government of an individual's encryption key is a powerful temptation to conduct an abusively expansive search. Such a key might give access not only to a certain set of e-mail conversations, but to every document in that holder's possession, and indeed, to all future communications encrypted with that key.

At present, there is no way to guarantee that the government could not use a key beyond a stipulated time limit; knowledge of a key cannot be "turned off' the way the telephone company terminates a wiretap that a court deems arbitrary. Although the simplest method for surveillance would be to gain access to the user's Internet service provider, it is theoretically possible, and indeed likely, that the United States government could tap e-mail by trapping the information packets that comprise any particular message at a large number of publicly accessible Internet nodes in the country. Foreign governments, of course, could simply tap the main line that connects their country to the rest of the world. Where governments can censor the Internet through these main lines, they can tap messages as well.

Human Rights Principles and Specific Policy Issues

Encryption is more than a shield for human rights activists. It is both a method and a subject of communication that is fully protected by the right of free expression, which is set forth not only in the First Amendment to the United States Constitution but also in

Article 19 of the International Covenant on Civil and Political Rights, to which the United States is a party. That international treaty provides in pertinent part:

> Everyone shall have the right to freedom of expression; this right shall include freedom to seek, receive and impart information and ideas of all kinds, regardless of frontiers, either orally, in writing or in print, in the form of art, or through any other media of his choice.

Speech expressed via the medium of the Internet is no less speech if it is encoded; it deserves the full protection of both international and constitutional law. Moreover, it is established in United States law that computer programs themselves are speech expressive of ideas, as evidenced by the fact they are protected by copyright, not patent. In particular, encryption programs are speech, as the federal court for the Northern District of California made clear last year in *Bernstein v. Department of State:* "Software relating to encryption is simply a topic of speech employed by some scientists involved in applied research. Hence Snuffle is speech afforded the full protection of the First Amendment not because it enables encryption, but because it is itself speech."

From this flows several conclusions. That language itself is part and parcel of expression is internationally accepted, and recognized in United States law. The use of encryption alone should not subject an individual to criminal sanction, any more than the use of Pig Latin or Swahili to communicate. The sorts of countries most eager to ban the use of encryption, such as China and Iran, are not known for respect of freedom of speech. Second, under the Covenant, the communication of encryption programs to others, regardless of frontiers, cannot be subject to a blanket ban, but may be restricted only as "necessary in a democratic society" for important government interests such as national security or public safety, narrowly construed.

The determination of necessity involves assessing whether the restriction is proportional in severity and intensity to the purpose being sought. For example, it would not be acceptable to merely invoke a general concern with national security or public safety as a justification to limit encryption; rather, the specific limitation would have to be weighed to test if it is the least restrictive means of securing the government interest.

Encryption is also an important bulwark against violations of privacy in an age where computerization and data banks enable the collection of huge amounts of personal information on individuals. Article 17(l) of the International Covenant on Civil and Political Rights provides:

No one shall be subjected to arbitrary or unlawful interference with his privacy, family, home or correspondence, nor to unlawful attacks on his honor and reputation.

The prohibition on arbitrary or unlawful interference covers surveillance techniques such as wiretaps and interception of Internet communication. The requirement that searches be lawful entails that they must be legally authorized in such a way as to give persons notice of what precise circumstances would warrant interference. In U.S. terms, the expectation of privacy in certain situations (and certainly communication via encryption is one such situation) cannot be casually breached. A search is arbitrary where it creates a disproportional burden on the rights of individuals given the threat to a state interest such as crime prevention. Searches in the context of a criminal investigation should be judicially supervised and of limited scope to prevent the unnecessary derogation of individual freedom. The United Nations Human Rights Committee, which is charged with interpreting the International Covenant on Civil and Political Rights, has stated that "Surveillance, whether electronic or otherwise ... should be prohibited," noting that the decision to use "authorized interference" must be made on "a case-by-case" basis.

Wiretaps have been criticized because they are to a certain extent indiscriminate, breaching the privacy of any caller connected to a specific telephone line that is under surveillance. To counter abuse, they are limited in duration and authorized only where there is a showing that other means would not produce the necessary evidence. Interception using private encryption keys presents an even greater potential to violate the rights of innocent interlocutors as it renders accessible every coded communication with a particular user, and not just those using a particular telephone line. Nor has the technological problem of "taking back" the key from the government been solved, should a law enforcement use be deemed unwarranted.

Alerting the key owner so that the key could be changed would expose and possibly compromise a criminal investigation, but keeping the key owner in the dark would give the government the ability to conduct an unlimited search. With regard to personal information held on computers or data banks, the United Nations Human Rights Committee has stipulated that every person should be able to "ascertain which public authorities or private individuals or bodies control or may control their files"

Moreover, international law requires the state not only to refrain from arbitrary interference with privacy, but to affirmatively protect everyone from such attacks. Any requirement that persons leave the keys to their encoded communications immediately raises the question of risk. Most information has a price; and much of what will be encrypted will be thought of as valuable information. It is hard to imagine that whatever certification is required for trustees of these keys, they will be in all cases impervious to corruption, or simple human error. Even assuming no failing on the part of the trustee, there is no reason that hackers, who seem able to breach the Department of Defense's computer network, will not try their hand at key repositories as well.

These risks cast doubt on whether key escrow, whether mandated or imposed through government pressure on the market, may compromise the ability of individuals to be safe from attacks on their privacy and reputation. Perhaps the most powerful fact in the entire encryption debate is that strong encryption is already available and in use worldwide. Restrictions on the export of programs that are already available abroad thus raises the prospect of suppression of speech in the face of prior disclosure, a practice condemned even where it is accepted that such speech indeed implicates national security.

The availability of strong encryption throws into question the actual utility of key recovery and export bans to law enforcement. There is no doubt that some criminals will use the less secure forms of communication, but the serious professional cartels and syndicates that populate the arguments of control advocates will no doubt go to the trouble to use the more secure technology, available now at trivial cost.

The issue is not whether key recovery would be useful to law enforcement — there is no doubt this is so. The question is, at what cost to the rights of millions of innocent individuals? Principles of human rights and criminal justice are premised on the idea that it is better that the guilty sometimes go free if that is necessary to protect the rights of the innocent. When the incremental utility of key recovery is weighed against the threat to speech and privacy of individuals worldwide, it is not at all clear that the balance is in favor of law enforcement.

The Modern Surveillance Society

Encryption debate goes to the heart of what sort of society Americans envisage for the twenty-first century. There are hints of an ominous trend in the government's efforts to pressure industry into designing infrastructure in a way that facilitates surveillance. Controversial digital telephony legislation was opposed by the industry and civil rights advocates because it forces the industry to adopt design features that facilitate wiretapping in a way that lends itself to over broad or abusive surveillance. It goes against the grain in this country to press industry into such a role. Who would not be repelled by the prospect of the government asking the hotel construction contractors to install listening devices in every new room, even if it promised never to use them except on a court order? Would you buy a home safe from a company that will send the combination to the local police on request?

The surveillance mentality is a characteristic of totalitarian states, such as the former Soviet Union, or China, where the individual's freedom invariably is subordinated in the name of public interest, variously defined by the powers of the day. The surveillance mechanisms of those regimes — internal travel documents, personal dossiers, household registration, work histories, family histories — are costly, requiring huge bureaucracies, continuous data collection and millions of informants.

Surveillance in the electronic age, however, can be done cheaply with a few people pressing a few buttons, capturing floods of data without the subject ever knowing. When we consider the risks posed to law and order from encryption, we must also weigh the prospect of government access to our private lives on an unimagined scale, and its potential to repress or inhibit free speech, not only within our borders but globally.

6

Internet: A Unique Communications Medium

The Internet represents a major development in enabling persons to communicate with others and to obtain information. Some have compared its importance to the invention of the printing press.

In the view of Human Rights Watch, the rights to freedom of expression, information, privacy, and free association under international law apply as much to online communication as to other forms of individual communication. While international treaties and instruments do not address electronic speech specifically, their assertion of the right to "seek, receive and impart information and ideas *through any media and regardless of frontiers*" (emphasis added) is clearly applicable to expression via the Internet.

Article 19 of the Universal Declaration of Human Rights proclaims:

Everyone has the right to freedom of opinion and expression; this right includes freedom to hold opinions without interference and to seek, receive and impart information and ideas through any media and regardless of frontiers.

Article 19 of the International Covenant on Civil and Political Rights (ICCPR) reaffirms that everyone's right to freedom of expression "shall include the freedom to seek, receive and impart information and ideas of all kinds, regardless of frontiers, either orally, in writing or in print, in the form of art, or through any other media of his choice." Article 19 states, furthermore, that restrictions on this right "shall only be such as are provided by law and are necessary: (a) For respect of the rights or reputations of others; (b) For the protection of national security or of public order (*ordre public*), or of public health or morals."(2) The ICCPR has been ratified by Algeria, Egypt, Iran, Iraq, Israel, Jordan, Lebanon, Kuwait, Libya, Morocco, Syria, Tunisia, and Yemen. It has not been ratified by Bahrain, Oman, Qatar, Saudi Arabia, and the United Arab Emirates.(3)

The Open Internet Policy Principles, declared in March 1997 by a working group of European and North American experts, point out:

The Internet does not exist in a legal vacuum. For the most part, existing laws can and should regulate conduct on the Internet to the same degree as other forms of conduct. Such laws may differ from country to country, but should conform with the applicable binding human rights obligations contained in the Universal Declaration of Human Rights, the International Covenant on Civil and Political Rights and the European Convention on Human Rights.

Under international law, governments are allowed to restrict the free flow of information to protect certain narrow interests such as national security or public morals. But any prior censorship of material before it is published should be subjected to the strictest level of scrutiny in line with international standards, which normally includes inquiry into the interest sought to be protected, the seriousness of the threat, and whether there are alternate means of protecting that interest that are less restrictive of the right to free expression.

Indeed, the American Convention on Human Rights states in Article 13 that the right to freedom of expression "shall not be subject to prior censorship." Filtering or blocking access to Internet material by a government amounts to pre-publication censorship. Virtually all governments in the Middle East that block content on the Internet suppress some material that is unquestionably legal. Moreover, none of the governments in the region make public how censorship is actually practiced and what sites are blocked, insulating their actions from any scrutiny or evaluation under international human rights standards. The decision of what to block, and what technology to use to block it, should be in the hands of end users, rather than governments. A variety of software programs is readily available to users for this purpose.

The Right to Privacy

The freedom from arbitrary and unlawful interference with one's privacy and correspondence is protected in international law, and applies to electronic communications. A capricious, unjust or disproportionate interference would be "arbitrary," as would one that was for a purpose inimical to the protection of human rights more generally, such as inhibiting peaceful dissent. States may not randomly or freely intercept or monitor e-mail or Internet usage; in the narrow circumstances where surveillance can be justified, it must be subject to limitation and control to avoid infringing these rights. Moreover, the International Covenant on Civil and Political Rights requires states to act positively to protect individuals from such interference with privacy or correspondence on the part of third parties such as non-state actors. Encryption, as a technology that protects communications and correspondence from arbitrary interference, should be lawful and accessible to individual users.

Free expression encompasses a right to communicate anonymously. Anonymity in communications is critical to the right to express political beliefs, and to seek and impart information without fear of retribution. Anonymity has served persons who wish to provide anonymous tips to journalists or "blow the whistle" on improprieties in their workplace, authors who wish to write under assumed names, and participants in sensitive discussions, such as an AIDS support group. The role of anonymous speech in fostering freedom of expression was eloquently defended thus:

Despite readers' curiosity and the public's interest in identifying the creator of a work of art, an author generally is free to decide whether or not to disclose her true identity. The decision in favor of anonymity may be motivated by fear of economic or official retaliation, by concern about social ostracism, or merely by a desire to preserve as much of one's privacy as possible. Whatever the motivation may be, at least in the field of literary endeavor, the interest in having anonymous works enter the marketplace of ideas unquestionably outweighs any public interest in requiring disclosure as a condition of entry.

Encryption

Encoding electronic communications (encryption) is growing more commonplace, and indeed, is commonly recognized as essential to facilitating the growth of electronic commerce. "Strong" encryption software, that is, coding that is nearly impossible for third parties to decipher, is widely available now to individuals and businesses, where once it was solely used by governments. Encryption protects privacy of communications, but even more importantly, it enables the free expression of ideas and information, particularly where there has been a record of government surveillance and repression. By guaranteeing privacy of communications and authenticating the identity of communicators, encryption also enables free association between individuals in cyberspace, an important extension of a traditional right in the new circumstances of globalization.

While there are legitimate law enforcement concerns that must be taken into account in any national policy on encryption, there is no justification for either banning individual use of encryption or licensing users. Encryption should be viewed as a vehicle of expression like a language; the use of encryption alone should not subject an individual to criminal sanction, any more than should the use of Esperanto or Swahili to communicate. Individuals should not be required to obtain authorization from the authorities in order to send or receive encrypted communications, nor should they be compelled to provide in advance to law enforcement authorities access to key recovery or other mechanisms that would permit the decoding of their communications. These are all over-broad policies that penalize law-abiding persons.

Liability for Online Content

The right to free expression is best served by laws that focus liability for speech on the originator of the offending content, rather than on its conduit. ISPs do not fit neatly into any existing media paradigm and should not be subjected to regulatory structures that may be suitable for other technologies or media, such as a newspaper that can be held liable for articles appearing in its pages. ISPs act most of the time merely as conduits of information (data carriers, akin to telephone companies), offering the technical means for users to receive and disseminate information. In most cases, ISPs have no knowledge of the content of the messages they transmit, or even of the web sites they host—many of which are revised daily by their authors. The situation is arguably different when the offending content is contained in material over which the ISP exercises editorial control, such as a proprietary opinion column; or when the ISP is made aware that offending content has been posted on a web site it hosts and does not remove it.

To hold ISPs presumptively liable for all content they host or carry would pose a regulatory burden on providers that would drastically reduce and slow the flow of information—if the burden could be carried at all. The Global Internet Liberty Campaign (GILC) argues,

"No one can monitor the enormous quantity of network traffic, which may consist of hundreds of thousands of e-mails, newsgroup messages, files, and Web pages that pass through in dozens of text and binary formats, some of them readable only by particular proprietary tools." Second, GILC points out, "ISPs cannot provide material in one country while blocking it in another; such a distinction would require an enormous new infrastructure on top of the current network."

The Johannesburg Principles on National Security, Freedom of Expression and Access to Information, put forward on October 1, 1995 by a group of experts in international law, national security, and human rights, state that restrictions on freedom of expression should be permitted only when "the government can demonstrate that the restriction is prescribed by law and is necessary in a democratic society to protect a legitimate national security interest".

According to the Principles, the burden of demonstrating the validity of the restriction rests with the government. Criticism of the government or its leaders is protected. In addition, a government must demonstrate that "the restriction imposed is the least restrictive means possible for protecting that interest".

The Universal Declaration of Human Rights affirms in Article 12, "No one shall be subjected to arbitrary interference with his privacy, family, home or correspondence." The International Covenant on Civil and Political Rights states in Article 17, "No one shall be subjected to arbitrary or unlawful interference with his privacy, family, home or correspondence..." The language of this provision is broad enough to encompass online communications, including electronic mail and newsgroup postings.

Encryption involves encoding a text prior to transmission, through the use of mathematical logarithms, so that it can be read only by the sender and the intended recipient, who are in possession of "keys" that decrypt the encoded text and present it in its original form.

Requiring that laws restricting the content of on-line speech distinguish between the liability of content providers and the liability of data carriers. Insisting that on-line free expression not be restricted by indirect means such as excessively restrictive governmental or private controls over computer hardware or software, telecommunications infrastructure, or other essential components of the Internet.

Including citizens in the Global Information Infrastructure (GII) development process from countries that are currently unstable economically, have insufficient infrastructure, or lack sophisticated technology. Prohibiting discrimination on the basis of race, color, sex, language, religion, political or other opinion, national or social origin, property, birth or other status. Ensuring that personal information generated on the Internet for one purpose is not used for an unrelated purpose or disclosed without the person's informed consent and enabling individuals to review personal information on the Internet and to correct inaccurate information. Allowing on-line users to encrypt their communications and information without restriction.

"Everyone has the right to freedom of opinion and expression; this right includes freedom to hold opinions without interference and to seek, receive and impart information and ideas through any media and regardless of frontiers."

Universal Declaration of Human Rights, Article 19 (emphasis added). For the first time since this 1948 proclamation of the international human right to freedom of expression, the citizens of the world have the ability to exercise that right on a truly global basis, "regardless of frontiers." With the advent of the Internet, methods of accessing and disseminating information have been fundamentally changed, with profound implications for individuals, civil society and governments.

Like no medium before it, the Internet permits any individual with a computer and a gateway to the Internet to communicate instantaneously with others worldwide. The Internet offers educational institutions, businesses, and non-profit organizations an opportunity to exchange ideas and promote scientific, cultural, and economic progress. Traditional forms of media can greatly expand their audiences at nominal cost. The Internet is global in its reach. To a degree that no other technology can, it transcends national borders and eliminates barriers to the free flow of information.

These unique features of this new technology, if properly supported, can foster the freedom of expression essential to democratic rule and civil society in ways previously impossible.

Governments, however, have already begun to impose controls on the Internet, threatening the potential of this new medium. Some governments have enacted laws prohibiting certain content on the Internet and have sought to prosecute users and service providers. Others have tried to control access, by insisting on the installation of national "proxy servers" and requiring the blocking of targeted web sites. And in other countries, governments have encouraged forms of "self-regulation" that are in fact intended to enlist service providers to control the behavior of their customers.

An increasingly well-established body of international law protects the right to freedom of expression. As we shall see, various human rights instruments are diluted by exceptions and may be difficult to enforce. Moreover, not all countries are parties to a binding human rights agreement. But international human rights law undoubtedly has advanced the cause of free expression and undoubtedly applies to the Internet and other digital media. Given the broad language of international and regional human rights documents, there is no doubt that government measures to control the Internet are subject to challenge under international law.

The purpose of this report is to lay the groundwork for the proposition that the unique qualities of the Internet support an even more robust application of international free expression principles to online communications. The technology itself both demands and can support fuller protection of free expression: The borderless nature of the Internet requires that the phrase "regardless of frontiers," which appears in the key international human rights instruments, be applied with a fresh eye. The concept of a right to "impart" information takes on new meaning when anyone can be a publisher.

Since censorship in one country may constitute a direct infringement on the right of persons in other countries to "impart" information "without regard to frontiers," the traditional deference given to local norms should be less relevant to the Internet. The decentralized nature of the Internet makes government controls less effective (even futile), because Internet users have numerous ways of circumventing them. At the same time, the user-controlled nature of the technology means that government controls are less necessary in some contexts. Furthermore, given the essentially unlimited capacity of the Internet, there is less need for government intervention to ensure fairness or balance or to protect reputation. On the Internet, the marketplace of ideas can function with less regulation since good ideas can always achieve the space they deserve. Mistakes can be corrected and the right of reply can be effectuated instantaneously. Under international law, necessity, proportionality, and efficacy are key concepts in judging the validity of restrictions on freedom of expression. If government regulation of content on the Internet is not likely to succeed and not necessary, then it becomes less supportable under international rules.

This paper is merely a beginning, intended to spark further action. A closer examination of the caselaw of the international tribunals is required. A fuller effort is needed to educate judges of the international tribunals, staff of the human rights commissions, and policymakers at international bodies on the unique elements of the Internet and the special significance of user control. Ultimately, free expression cases involving the Internet will be brought before the international human rights tribunals. With further development of the principles outlined here, the Internet could serve as a fulcrum for the expansion of free expression principles.

This chapter is addressed both to governments and to Internet activists. To governments, it says, "Don't try to censor the Internet because your efforts may well violate international human rights law, especially given the unique nature of the Internet." To activists, the chapter says, "Consider how to use international human rights documents to challenge Internet censorship. Here are some arguments why the Internet is entitled to even greater protection that other media."

Applying international human rights principles to the Internet requires an appreciation of the fundamental characteristics of the digital on-line media. The unique qualities of the Internet justify according the strongest protection to free expression on-line and should prompt a new vision of the right to receive and impart information "regardless of frontiers."

The Internet is really a network of networks and is comprised of a number of different technologies and infrastructures. Viewed as a whole, it is uniquely:

Global: The Internet provides immediate access to information from around the world. With simple e-mail, it is as easy to send a message to another continent as it is to the building next door. Through the World Wide Web, thousands of newspapers and tens of thousands of other information sources are available from around the world. While access is still not available to most of the world's population, the fastest rates of growth are in less developed countries.

Decentralized: The Internet was designed by purpose to be decentralized, to work without gatekeepers, and to accommodate multiple, competitive access points. The absence of gatekeepers of the kind that exist in broadcasting, cable television, or satellite transmission, the availability of numerous hosting sites, and the irrelevance of geographic location mean that material can almost always be published outside the control of governments, monopolies or oligopolies.

Open: The Internet has low barriers to access. Service can be priced very inexpensively. The costs of creating and disseminating content are extremely low. Because of the Internet, anybody who has a computer and a modem can be a publisher — a digital Gutenberg.

Abundant: The digitization of information and the ability to transmit it over the telephone network, combined with the decentralized nature of the Internet, mean that the Internet has essentially unlimited capacity to hold information. In economic terms, the marginal cost of adding another web site, sending another email message, or posting to a newsgroup is essentially zero.

Interactive: The Internet is designed for bi-directional communication: All Internet users can be both speakers and listeners. The Internet allows responsive communication from one-to-one, from one-to-many, and from many-to-one.

User-Controlled: The Internet allows users to exercise far more choice than even cable television or short wave radio. The user can skip from site to site in ways that are not dictated by the content providers or by the access provider. User can control what content reaches their computers. Users can encrypt their communications to hide them from government censors.

Infrastructure independent: The Internet is not linked to any infrastructure other than the telephone system. Dial-up access is available from any telephone that can make an international call. Access to the Internet can also be wireless and satellite based and therefore further removed from effective control of governments.

Courts and other institutions that have considered in depth the question of Internet regulation have recognized these unique features. In a 1996 Communication, the European Commission noted: "A unique characteristic of the Internet is that it functions simultaneously as a medium for publishing and for communication. Unlike in the case of traditional media, the Internet supports a variety of communication modes: one-to-one, one-to-many, many-to-many. An Internet user may "speak" or "listen" interchangeably. At any given time, a receiver can and does become content provider, of his own accord, or through "re-posting" of content by a third party. The Internet therefore is radically different from traditional broadcasting. It also differs radically from a traditional telecommunication service."

The European Commission Legal Advisory Board, which advises the European Commission on legal matters concerning the European information market, also recognized the uniqueness of the Internet, calling it "a positive instrument, empowering citizens and educators, lowering the barriers to the creation and distribution of content and offering universal access to ever richer sources of digital information." The United States Supreme Court, in ruling that the Communications Decency Act was unconstitutional and that the Internet merited the strongest protection of free expression, based its judgment on the conclusion that the Internet was "a unique and wholly new medium of worldwide human communication."

The vast new potential of the Internet for expanding access to information and participation in government and civil society has already begun to show itself with concrete contributions to democracy and human rights.

Facilitating participation in government

The bi-directional nature of the Internet has tremendous potential for fostering democratic participation, giving voice to the voiceless. The Internet could allow citizens to communicate with their government, to pose questions to their elected representatives, and to submit comments on pending issues.

While many governments have been slow to take advantage of the democratic potential of the Internet, some harbingers of progress can be seen. In January 1995, the municipality of Bologna created the Iperbole system — a free-of-charge "civic network" offering citizens and businesses an opportunity to send requests, suggestions, claims and complaints by email to more than 1,300 municipal offices. The system also includes discussion and newsgroups dealing with specific topics, suggested by citizens, business enterprises, public and private institutions, and by the municipal administration itself. The UK conducted a one-time on-line consultation on the government's freedom of information proposal.

Western governments are not the only ones that have begun to respond. In Hungary earlier this year, Hungary's iNteRNeTTo held an online debate between politicians from the two leading parties. The Costa Rican government, to make voting more convenient, is working to shift to an electronic voting system. Taking advantage of a literacy rate of 94% and the fact that about 50% of grade schools have Internet-connected computers, Costa Rica hopes to run an entirely electronic balloting in 2002. International bodies also use the Internet to promote public participation in their activities. For example, last year the EU conducted an online forum regarding illegal or harmful content on the Internet.

Grassroots organizations can use the Internet to mobilize voters to be active on issues. One example is the Adopt your Legislator campaign developed by CDT in the US.

Expanding access to government information

One of the most important potential benefits of the Internet is the ability to provide rapid access to the full text of government documents. If a government is willing, it can provide its citizens access to enacted and proposed laws, regulations, government reports and statistics, transcripts of parliamentary debates, judicial decisions, all searchable by word or concept. Information previously available only to experts, usually only in the capital city, and often only with great expenditure of time and money can now be made available to individuals in the smallest rural town and at public libraries in the poorest neighborhoods. This vast openness need not be the luxury of only wealthy nations. In almost every country in the world, most government information is now created by word processing, meaning that the information is already digitized. Again, if the government is willing, the information can be rapidly and inexpensively put on-line, even using simple Gopher technology.

Many nations have begun to use the Internet, nations as diverse as the United Kingdom, the Czech Republic, and South Africa. The European Union is a most effective user of the Web to make its voluminous publications available to a wide audience. Some examples from the U.S. include THOMAS, the Website of the Library of Congress and GPO Access providing access to materials from the Government Printing Office, including all proposed federal regulations, and transcripts of daily Congressional debates.

Civil society through the building of networks among individuals

The Internet has opened up new opportunities for discourse, on matters political, intellectual, and personal. The Internet's architecture allows for a diversity of views and exchange of information that is simply not possible in any other media. As of August 1998, one service identified 29,000 IRC (Internet Relay Chat) channels, 30,000 Usenet newsgroups, and 90,095 mailings lists — each one representing a network of individuals worldwide interested in a particular subject.

Among the first to use the Internet were human rights activists. In 1992, the International Freedom of Expression eXchange (IFEX) was established to provide accurate and timely information regarding censorship and attacks on journalists. The primary method of transmitting information is by e-mail: whenever there is a serious threat to freedom of expression, the IFEX action alert network sends out detailed information on the case via e-mail to participating organizations and individuals, who in turn mount international protests from their own regions. GILC member "Derechos" is an on-line human rights organization focusing on Latin America that exists largely through the Internet.

The Internet has been at the forefront of democratic uprisings. In Indonesia, "Bypassing the government-controlled television and radio stations, dissidents shared information about protests by e-mail, inundated news groups with stories of President Suharto's corruption, and used chat groups to exchange tips about resisting troops."

Traditional media and promoting pluralism

The Web has become a place where there is ready access to newspapers and other publications. A wide range of print publications are available on-line, and many broadcast media now have on-line services that allow searching of past broadcasts, a capability previously available cnly to governments and a few research institutes. The Radio Free Europe/Radio Liberty Newsline illustrates the use of old-fashioned e-mail to disseminate information to a dispersed audience very inexpensively.

The Internet makes it possible for more organizations to distribute news and commentary, increasing the diversity of voices. The Association for Independent Media in Bosnia has made use of the Internet, both e-mail and the World Wide Web. AIM operates on the principle of a mail-box system. Information is exchanged via a central computer located in Paris. AIM texts are available in Serbian, Croatian, Bosnian, and a choice of texts is available in English. Subscribers to AIM regularly receive the whole production of AIM via e-mail. The China News Digest makes available news from non-official sources. While the site is sometimes blocked by the Chinese government, users in China have found ways to access it. The service also uses e-mail to disseminate its news within China.

The Internet is Uniquely Resistant to Government Controls

With the Internet, it is increasingly difficult for governments to control content. The Internet offers creative ways to disseminate information around the controls of censors. Radio B92 in Belgrade is one of the leading examples of this. When authorities shut down the radio station, it put its programming on the Internet through RealAudio, using a Dutch service provider; Radio Free Europe, Voice of America, and Deutche Welle picked up the station off the Net and rebroadcast it back into Serbia, where it served as the source of independent reporting and a focal point for democratic opposition. Faced with this strategy, the government allowed the station back on the air.

In June of 1997, Chinese dissidents founded *Tunnel*, a Chinese language journal of dissent. Tunnel is managed and edited in China. Once an issue is ready to be published, it is secretly delivered to the United States and then emailed back to China from an anonymous address. "Thus its staff remains safely hidden in cyberspace, and all of its contributors, both in China and abroad, write under pseudonyms."

The Digital Freedom Network, was created with the primary objective of publishing on-line material that has been suppressed. When the government of Belarus suppressed the independent newspaper Svaboda, Radio Free Europe/Radio Liberty made its reports available in three different ways: the Belarus service of RFE/RL featured materials from Svaboda journalists, its website posted their articles, and the daily live RealAudio news broadcast of RFE/RL's Belarus service carried Svaboda content.

The technology of the Internet frustrates control in other ways. Proxy servers purportedly block access to web sites known to contain objectionable content and thus preclude such content from being accessed. Such servers fail to achieve their goal, however, because web site operators whose sites are targeted as containing undesirable content can simply change their web site address; and an Internet user in a country imposing controls can simply dial into a server outside the country and access the desired information, thereby avoiding the proxy server altogether.

An "Anti-Censorship Proxy" has been created that allows users to evade filters. Even if the telephone company is state-owned, it cannot differentiate a telephone call to a foreign server from an international fax. Furthermore, encryption allows determined users to create "tunnels" to banned foreign sites in ways that completely evade government control. And while access through an Internet Service Provider is desirable, dial-up access is available from any telephone that can make an international call. Access to the Internet can also be wireless, making it even harder for governments to exercise controls.

The creation of mirror sites is one practice that helps assure the free flow of information, even against government censorship efforts. Given the global nature of the Internet, content can be published from anywhere in the world. When a government tries to prosecute a content provider or force the withdrawal of material, there are others around the world prepared to copy or mirror the information on their own sites, in countries where the information is legal.

One example involved the site of a Basque organization hosted by an American service provider. The site was supporting Basque independence, although it did not promote violence. Nonetheless, from Spain, there came an apparently orchestrated campaign of "mailbombing" — flooding the site's service provider with e-mail in order to disrupt service. The service provider publicized the problem and soon a number of organizations, one in Holland, one in England, several in the U.S., installed mirror websites, which were perfectly legal in the host country.

With so many sites, the harassment campaign fizzled out. The Internet Freedom Campaign, an English group hosting one of the mirror sites, set up an on-line bulletin board for surfers to post their opinions about the issue, showing how the Net is the perfect place for controversial information to appear, Similarly, when a local governmental body in the UK, the Nottinghamshire County Council, sought to suppress the publication of the so-called JET Report, an official report on the hysteria that has attended certain child abuse cases, the report was immediately mirrored on numerous sites, ultimately totaling 35, as a result of a campaign organized by GILC member Cyber-Rights & Cyber-Liberties (UK), When an issue of a Zambian newspaper carrying an article critical of the government was banned, the issue was mirrored outside the country.

Governments Have Sought to Impose Various Controls on Internet Content and Access

Despite the power of the Internet — or perhaps because of that very power — governments have sought to restrict it. Government actions infringing freedom of expression on the Internet take many forms:

— *Internet-specific laws:* Some governments have criminalized certain types of speech on the Internet. Such criminal penalties may come in the form of laws whose expressed intent is to protect minors from certain material regarded as "harmful." However, as the United States Supreme Court recently found, requiring that Internet speakers shield certain populations from their speech is effectively a total ban on that speech.

— *Application of existing laws:* Governments can act to restrict speech without specifically enacting laws targeting Internet-based speech. For example, German government action against CompuServe for providing access to material illegal under German law did not require enactment of new law, merely the assertion by government agents that certain Internet speech violated the existing laws.

— *Content-based license terms applied to Internet users and service providers:* Several countries have already established licensing systems that require Internet users and/or service providers to agree to refrain from certain kinds of speech, or block access to speech as a condition of having a license to use the Internet or provide access to the Net. China has issued rules requiring anyone with Internet access to refrain from proscribed speech. And the Singapore Broadcasting Authority requires all Internet Service Providers to abide by licensing terms demanding that they block access to foreign web sites and newsgroups deemed harmful to national morals.

— *Compelled use of filtering, rating or content labeling tools:* Blocking, filtering, and labeling techniques can prevent individuals from using the Internet to exchange information on topics that may be controversial or unpopular, enable the development of country profiles to facilitate a global/universal rating system desired by some governments, block access to content on entire domains, block access to Internet content available at any domain or page which contains a specific key word or character string in the address, and over-ride self-rating labels provided by content creators and providers. Where any such mechanisms are required by public authorities or otherwise forced on users, they constitute serious threats to human rights.

Regional Agreements Manifest a Universal Commitment to the Right to Free Expression

Over the past half-century, international human rights law has enshrined the rights to free expression, access to information, and privacy of communications, creating a strong presumption against governmental intrusions. These rights are reflected both in the provisions of numerous international and regional agreements and in decisions rendered by human rights tribunals. These human rights doctrines protecting freedom of expression are fully applicable to the Internet. Indeed, these protections may offer especially strong protection to the Internet, given its unique features.

These human rights instruments have their limitations. The Universal Declaration has been accepted in effect by all 185 Member States of the United Nations, but not all of its provisions have become binding. The International Covenant on Civil and Political Rights is binding, but its enforcement mechanisms are limited. While there are binding regional agreements for the Americas, for Europe, and for Africa, there are none for Asia or the Middle East. Enforcement mechanisms are available under these regional agreements, but they are limited too. Where individual review is available, the time required to pursue a case all the way to the international level may be substantial. Most importantly, these instruments, particularly the European Convention, are burdened with exceptions that have been seriously criticized as over-broad.

Nonetheless, these human rights agreements have served to expand freedom of expression worldwide, becoming part of international law and affecting the domestic laws of many nations. The numerous international and regional instruments discussed herein provide substantial evidence that the principle of free expression is a well-settled principle of international law. The collection of treaties, agreements, and international tribunal decisions also evidences an international consensus on the scope of this right: it applies to all forms of media, it applies to the ability to receive and to impart information, and it is subject to only limited restrictions.

The advent of the Internet raises the question of how these human rights instruments apply to the new communications media. The answers are in some respects encouraging: the instruments are drafted with very forward-looking language, with powerful implications for a medium that operates "regardless of frontiers."

International Agreements

The international community has stated its commitment to the right to free expression in a series of fundamental agreements, including the Universal Declaration of Human Rights, the International Covenant on Civil and Political Rights, and the International Covenant on Economic, Social and Cultural Rights.

Universal Declaration of Human Rights

The right of free expression was first proclaimed an international norm by the then-members of the United Nations in the 1948 Universal Declaration of Human Rights ("Universal Declaration"). Taken together, Articles 19, 12, and 27 of the Universal Declaration constitute a blueprint for the protection of free expression on the Internet.

Article 19 of the Universal Declaration proclaims: "Everyone has the right to freedom of opinion and expression; this right includes freedom to hold opinions without interference and to seek, receive and impart information and ideas through any medium and regardless of frontiers."

Article 12 of the Universal Declaration provides: *"No one shall be subjected to arbitrary interference with his privacy, family, home or correspondence."* The language of this provision is broad enough to encompass all communications directed to an individual or group of individuals, including electronic mail and newsgroup communications. Finally, the right to seek, receive and impart information guaranteed in Article 19 of the Universal Declaration is reinforced by Article 27, which upholds the right of each individual *"freely to participate in the cultural life of the community, to enjoy the arts and to share in scientific advancement and its benefits."* Given that the Internet's roots are in the exchange of scientific information, Article 27 seems particularly apt to the protection of communications on the Internet.

The foresightful language of Article 19 (*"through any medium"*) makes it clearly applicable to expression via the Internet. The rights to "seek" and "impart" information seem particularly relevant to "surfing" the 'Net and posting information on Web sites for all to read, while the right to "receive" information encompasses the exchange of electronic mail and the downloading of information.

The Universal Declaration is subject to exceptions. Article 29(2) provides:

"In the exercise of his rights and freedoms, everyone shall be subject only to such limitations as are determined by law solely for the purpose of securing due recognition and respect for the rights and freedoms of others and of meeting the just requirements of morality, public order and the general welfare in a democratic society."

Enforcement

The Universal Declaration is not a treaty. It was adopted by the United Nations General Assembly as a resolution having no force of law on its own. However, over time the Declaration has become a normative instrument that creates some legal obligations for Member States of the UN. Many of the principles established by the Universal Declaration have since entered the corpus of international law as evidenced by an overwhelming consensus of opinion and practice among states. This consensus is illustrated in subsequent international and regional treaties and agreements, decisions of international tribunals, and domestic constitutions and legislation. Further, the Declaration has served as an inspiration for other human rights agreements of more direct effect.

The United Nations Commission on Human Rights was created in 1946 under Article 68 of the UN Charter. States name representatives to the 53 member Commission, where they serve as instructed governmental delegates. The Commission prepares reports and coordinates an expansive network of working groups and rapporteurs with thematic or country mandates. It has been criticized for being politically motivated and selective in approach, but it serves as the principal UN forum for addressing charges of human rights violations and as a focal point for broadening the human rights agenda of the UN.

In 1993, the Commission established the position of Special Rapporteur on the promotion and protection of the right to freedom of opinion and expression. In his 1998 report to the Commission, the Special Rapporteur specifically commented on the impact of new communications technologies and governmental efforts to regulate them:

"The Special Rapporteur is of the opinion that the new technologies and, in particular, the Internet are inherently democratic, provide the public and individuals with access to information sources and enable all to participate actively in the communication process. The Special Rapporteur also believes that action by States to impose excessive regulations on the use of these technologies and, again, particularly the Internet, on the grounds that control, regulation and denial of access are necessary to preserve the moral fabric and cultural identity of societies is paternalistic.

These regulations presume to protect people from themselves and, as such, they are inherently incompatible with the principles of the worth and dignity of each individual. These arguments deny the fundamental wisdom of individuals and societies and ignore the capacity and resilience of citizens, whether on a national, State, municipal, community or even neighbourhood level, often to take self-correcting measures to re-establish equilibrium without excessive interference or regulation by the State."

In its resolution of April 1998 on the right to freedom of expression, the Commission welcomed the Special Rapporteur's report and specifically invited him to "assess the advantages and challenges of new telecommunications technologies, including the Internet, on the exercise of the right to freedom of opinion and expression,... taking into account the work undertaken by the Committee on the Elimination of Racial Discrimination on racism, racial discrimination, xenophobia, and related intolerance."

International Covenant on Civil and Political Rights

The principles first enunciated in the Universal Declaration are reiterated and expanded upon in the 1966 International Covenant on Civil and Political Rights ("ICCPR"), which took effect in 1976 and has now been ratified by 140 nations. Article 19 of the ICCPR restates

Article 19 of the Universal Declaration almost verbatim. It declares: *"Everyone shall have the right to hold opinions without interference. ... Everyone shall have the right to freedom of expression... ."* In words somewhat more expansive than the Universal Declaration, Article 19 of the ICCPR expressly states that the freedom of expression extends to all forms of media: *"this right shall include freedom to seek, receive and impart information and ideas of all kinds, regardless of frontiers, either orally, in writing or in print, in the form of art, or through any other media of his choice."* The ICCPR also reiterates the crux of Article 12 of the Universal Declaration: *"No one shall be subjected to arbitrary or unlawful interference with his privacy, family, home or correspondence."*

The ICCPR defines the scope of limitations that could be imposed on the freedom of expression. Consistent with the law of most if not all nations, the ICCPR recognizes that freedom of expression may be curtailed under certain circumstances. The ICCPR requires, however, that restrictions on free speech be narrowly defined and not arbitrary. Article 19(3) of the ICCPR provides that restrictions on the freedom of expression are valid only where such restrictions are *"provided by law and are necessary: a. For respect of the rights or reputation of others; [or] b. For the protection of national security or of public order, or of public health or morals."*

The essence of applying the ICCPR involves interpreting this limitation. It has been urged that this provision means that laws restricting freedom of expression must be "accessible, unambiguous, drawn narrowly, and with precision." Moreover, the burden of demonstrating the validity of a restriction on free speech should lie with the government. The key hurdle for governments is the requirement that restrictions be "necessary;" this has generally been interpreted as a high standard.

The ICCPR includes several other provisions relevant to freedom of expression. Article 17 provides, *"No one shall be subjected... to unlawful attacks on his honour and reputation. ... Everyone has the right to the protection of the law against such... attacks."* Article 20 states, *"Any advocacy of national, racial, or religious hatred that constitutes incitement to discrimination, hostility or violence shall be prohibited by law."*

Under the Covenant, States Parties are required to submit reports every five years on the measures they have taken to protect and advance human rights. The Covenant established a Human Rights Committee, one of the principal functions of which is to examine these reports. The Committee makes conclusions on individual state reports and also issues general comments, which serve as advisory opinions on the Covenant. (The Committee also has had since its inception jurisdiction over complaints filed by one State Party against another, but few states declared their acceptance of the mechanism and it has never been used).

In 1976, an optional protocol went into force which enables private parties to file individual complaints against States Parties that have ratified the covenant. The protocol is itself a treaty, and therefore binds the states that have ratified it. Complainants must exhaust domestic remedies first. Once a complaint has been admitted as properly drawn, the Committee brings the matter to the attention of the state involved, which has six months to respond. The Committee, after considering all the written communications on the matter, issues its "views."

The Committee has no power to enforce its findings, but it does require States Parties to indicate in their periodic reports what measures they have taken to give effect to the Committee's recommendations. "In particular, the State Party should indicate what remedy it has afforded the author of the communication whose rights the Committee has found to have been violated."

Economic, Social and Cultural Rights

Restrictions on the Internet also implicate rights established by the International Covenant on Economic, Social, and Cultural Rights ("ICESCR"). Echoing Article 27 of the Universal Declaration, Article 15 of the ICESCR recognizes the important *"benefits to be derived from the encouragement and development of international contacts and cooperation in the scientific and cultural fields."* Accordingly, the 136 signatories pledge to *"diffuse science and culture"* and to *"respect the freedom indispensable for scientific research and creative activity."* These provisions articulate that free expression across borders must be respected to realize social, scientific, and cultural advancements.

To take advantage of such progress, Article 15 of the ICESCR establishes that all individuals are entitled "to enjoy the benefits of scientific progress and its applications." One of the most effective means of doing so is through Internet communication, which enables people in distant and diverse countries to share valuable scientific research and social insights.

The ICESCR does not establish any interstate or individual complaint system. It only requires the States Parties to submit *"reports on the measures which they have adopted and the progress made in achieving the observance of the rights recognized herein."* Art. 16(1). There is a Committee on Economic, Social and Cultural Rights, which reviews the country reports and issues General Comments and analyses, which serve as a platform for the Committee to try to advance awareness of human rights issues arising in the social context.

Regional Agreements

Regional human rights agreements in Europe, the Americas, and Africa establish the right of free expression for all individuals and privacy in their communications with others. Such freedoms are protected in all forms of media and "regardless of frontiers." These regional agreements are especially important because of the opportunities they offer for international judicial review of actions restricting free expression.

European Convention of Human Rights

The European Convention for the Protection of Human Rights and Fundamental Freedoms ("European Convention") was adopted in 1950 by members of the Council of Europe. Article 10 states in full:

— "Everyone has the right to freedom of expression. This right shall include freedom to hold opinions and to receive and impart information and ideas without interference by public authority and regardless of frontiers. This Article shall not prevent States from requiring licensing of broadcasting, television or cinema enterprises.

— "The exercise of these freedoms, since it carries with it duties and responsibilities, may be subject to such formalities, conditions, restrictions or penalties as are prescribed by law and are necessary in a democratic society, in the interests of national security, territorial integrity or public safety, for the prevention of disorder or crime, for the protection of health or morals, for the protection of the reputation or rights of others, for preventing the disclosure of information received in confidence, or for maintaining the authority and impartiality of the judiciary."

The European Convention thus establishes that the right of free expression pertains to cross-border communication, which naturally applies to much of the content available on the Internet. Closely linked to freedom of expression are additional rights in the European Convention: the right to respect for correspondence and privacy, contained in Article 8; the right to freedom of peaceful assembly and freedom of association, contained in Article 11; and the right to manifest one's religion or belief, contained in Article 9.

Article 10 is not stated in absolute terms. The second paragraph specifies that freedom of expression can be curtailed in furtherance of a series of enumerated interests. It has been widely debated whether these exceptions are too broad. But even in the U.S. and other countries with constitutional free speech provisions, restrictions are permitted through judicial interpretation. Supporters of Article 10's approach argue that Article 10 is preferable because the catalogue of possible restrictions is limited and because Article 10 also establishes that any restriction on the exercise of the freedom of expression must be "prescribed by law" and "necessary in a democratic society" to serve one of the enumerated interests.

Application of the exceptions in the second paragraph will always turn on the factual and legal context, considered case by case. In specific situations, it has been found that there was no violation of Article 10 in: the application of blasphemy laws to seize a film, the UK's ban on broadcasting interviews with representatives of the IRA, prohibitions on Nazi material, laws against obscenity, even state disciplinary measures against a lawyer who used aggressive or insulting language.

Article 10 must be interpreted in light of other Articles, notably Article 17, which states that nothing in the Convention creates a right to engage in activities *"aimed at the destruction of any of the rights or freedoms set forth in the convention."* Article 17, it has been held, was intended "to prevent totalitarian groups from exploiting, in their own interests, the principles enunciated in the convention." Accordingly, for example, the Court has concluded that it was not a violation of the Convention for the Netherlands to convict extremist right-wing Dutch politicians for distributing racist leaflets. Other provisions affecting the freedom of expression include Article 6, which guarantees the right to a fair trial, and the right to personal privacy in Article 8, which protects a person's honor and reputation against attack, both of which concepts are also reflected in Article 10(2) itself.

Most European countries that are party to the Convention have made it part of their national law, meaning that it can be invoked in the national courts. For many years, the UK declined to do this, but the Convention will be fully incorporated in UK law when the Human Rights Bill 1998 is enacted.

The European Convention has an explicit enforcement mechanism based on judicial review by an independent regional tribunal, the European Court of Human Rights, located in Strasbourg. The most important feature of the Court's jurisdiction is that individuals can bring complaints against Contracting States alleging violations of the Convention. The procedures of the Court are well beyond the scope of this paper. It is sufficient to note that individuals may bring their cases before the Court after exhausting local remedies and that an application must first be presented to the European Commission on Human Rights. The Commission decides on the admissibility of the complaint. If the Commission decides that the case is admissible, it issues a report (which is not binding), and there is a procedure for referring cases to the Court. The Court's judgments on the merits are binding but declaratory in nature. The Court has no power to quash the impugned decisions of the national authorities. The Court may, however, award "just satisfaction" in the form of financial compensation. In most cases, States have been reasonably swift to make the changes in their laws and practices necessary to bring them into conformity with the Court's decision.

Case Law of the European Court Relevant to the Internet

The European Court described the scope and importance of the right of free expression under Article 10 in its landmark decision in *Handyside v. UK:*

— "Freedom of expression constitutes one of the essential foundations of [a democratic society], one of

> the basic conditions for its progress and for the development of every man. Subject to paragraph 2 of Article 10, it is applicable not only to 'information' or 'ideas' that are favourably received or regarded as inoffensive or as a matter of indifference, but also to those that offend, shock or disturb the State or any sector of the population. Such are the demands of that pluralism, tolerance and broadmindedness without which there is no democratic society."

The Court applies a three-part test. Any restriction on the freedom of expression must be prescribed by law; have as its aim a goal that is legitimate under paragraph 2 of Article 10; and be "necessary in a democratic society" to achieve that goal. The Court has stated that the exceptions in paragraph 2 "must be narrowly interpreted and the necessity for any restrictions must be convincingly established."

At the same time, the Court has concluded that states are allowed a "margin of appreciation" to determine whether a restriction is necessary in light of local circumstances. This means that what can be prohibited can vary from country to country. This is particularly true in the area of morals. Thus, in the *Handyside* case, the Court held that it was permissible for the UK to prosecute the publisher and seize and destroy copies of a certain book even though the book was acceptable in most other countries. In *Sunday Times v. UK*, the court found that states were not entitled to such a margin of deference regarding the "far more objective notion of the 'authority' of the judiciary."

Much of the interpretation of Article 10 turns on the interplay between the concept of "appreciation" and the requirement that any restriction be "necessary in a democratic society." The unique elements of the Internet require a reconsideration of both concepts.

The Court has made it clear that the free expression principles of Article 10 apply differently to different media. The nature and extent of permissible restrictions depends on the nature of the medium. In particular, "the potential impact of the medium concerned is an important factor" to be considered in applying Article 10. The Court has noted that material that might not be proper for broadcast could not be banned from print. The Internet, for all its power, tends to be a less immediate, less inflammatory medium. For example, offensive or heated language that would pose a threat to public order in front of a crowd poses no danger on the Internet when readers are dispersed in location and may even be dispersed over time.

The necessity test has several elements: First, the European Court has made it clear that any government action must be effective, in that it must be reasonably likely to in fact serve one of the permitted governmental interests. Second, the Court has made it clear that any restriction must be proportional, meaning that it cannot be overbroad. Third, the concept of proportionality implies that a government restriction should not be permitted if a less restrictive alternative would serve the same goal while respecting other values such as the primacy of the family.

Various forms of government Internet censorship would violate Article 10 under one or more of these tests. First, none of the proposed methods of control (short of denying access to the Internet altogether) are likely to be effective, given the very nature of the Internet. Users will almost always be able to find ways around the censor, both to post banned material and to access it. As demonstrated by the examples of mirroring and anti-censorship given the borderless nature of the Internet, a user in a repressive country can usually find a host in another country that will host banned content. In addition, to further protect themselves from government controls, speakers can render themselves anonymous/ unidentifiable. Efforts to block offensive material at the national level have proven to be very spotty at best — even the simple changing of a URL can frustrate a filter. Unencrypted email is extremely difficult to filter, while it is absolutely impossible to filter email if it is encrypted, even at a very low level of security.

Government censorship also will not meet the proportionality test. For example, government bans on information deemed harmful to minors will result in making the same information unavailable to adults, who are entitled to see it.

Finally, in some contexts, the user-controlled nature of the Internet makes government control unnecessary because user control offers alternative means of achieving certain goals. This point could be especially relevant in the area of protection of morals, where the Court has granted states the widest margin of appreciation. Many of the proposed governmental controls on content on the Internet are put forth in the name of protecting children from content that is permissible for adults. But the unique user-controlled nature of the Internet makes government control for this purpose unnecessary, because parents are in a better position than the government to control what their children see, by supervision, training, and, if they chose, by using filtering software. While the use of filtering, labeling and rating tools raises serious freedom of expression concerns, both the US Supreme Court and the European Commission have relied on the availability of filtering software as a reason not to pursue governmental censorship.

This argument does not assume that filtering is effective. GILC members have documented the flaws in various filtering programs, including their overbroad blocking of perfectly appropriate material. So this argument is not in any way an endorsement of filtering software. Further, any government-mandated filtering by schools, libraries or ISPs is censorship and would violate the free expression principles discussed here. See section V.C below. The argument here simply recognizes that filtering software is available to users. Families can use it if they want. If government tried to require families to use it, that would constitute impermissible censorship and probably infringe on other human rights principles protecting the sanctity of the family. But the values supposedly promoted by government censorship in the area of protecting children are already reflected in products available to the end user. The fact that filtering is available to individuals is not a reason for the government to mandate its use; rather, under free expression principles, the availability of filtering software to parents is one reason why governments should not mandate it or otherwise restrict expression on the Internet. It is not necessary for governments to regulate the Internet to protect children because parents can exercise control.

A family's choice to use filtering preserves their moral values without limiting the options of other users. Since there is an alternative means of satisfying the government's goal that also empowers families, the government restriction on speech should violate Article

10. Particularly relevant to the Internet, given the practice of mirroring, are a number of Court decisions holding that prohibition on publishing certain content was not "necessary in a democratic society" if the information was otherwise available. Perhaps the most important case on this subject is the famous "Spycatcher" case, involving the memoirs of a former member of the British Security Service.

The Court held that the injunction against publishing the book was no longer appropriate under Article 10 after the book was published in the United States. (It is noteworthy that the government's interest lost its force when the information was published in another country.) From that point on, since the confidentiality had been breached, the injunction in the UK violated Article 10. In *Weber v. Switzerland,* the Court unanimously found that the sentencing of Mr. Weber to a fine for having breached, at a press conference, the confidentiality of a judicial investigation was not "necessary" for the protection and impartiality of the judiciary because the information had already been disclosed at a prior press conference. In *Vereniging Weekblad Bluf! v. the Netherlands,* the Court followed the same approach with regard to the seizure and withdrawal from circulation of a magazine article on the activities of the Internal Security Services of the Netherlands.

In that case, after the magazine had been seized, the publishers quickly reprinted a large number of copies and sold them on the streets of Amsterdam. Since the information in question had already been made public, the Court concluded that preventing its disclosure was not "necessary in a democratic society." While there was a dispute as to the number of people to whom the information had been made accessible, the court noted that those people "were able in their turn to communicate it to others."

The Court has also recognized a distinction between those who make certain offensive statements, and those who serve as the conduits for that information to the public. The distinction arose in a case concerning the liability of a journalist, but it may have relevance to the question of ISP liability. The Court said that a journalist could not be prosecuted for publishing racist remarks uttered by others. The Court said: "The punishment of a journalist for assisting in the dissemination of statements made by another person in an interview would seriously hamper the contribution of the press to discussion of matters of public interest and should not be envisaged unless there are particularly strong reasons for doing so." Substitute "ISP" for "journalist" or "the press" and one has a good statement of the importance of not holding ISPs liable for content they did not create. Other cases has also drawn a distinction between the author of statements and the conveyor of those statements.

Finally, in *Informationsverein Lentia v. Austria,* the Court concluded that Contracting States are under a positive obligation under Article 10 to take measures to ensure pluralism in the media. The case concerned applicants to set up a radio station and a television station. In Austria, that right was vested solely in the Austrian Broadcasting Authority. The Court found that as a result of technical progress, restrictions in the form of a public monopoly could no longer be justified and therefore violated Article 10.

The Court has decided very few cases based on Article 10's right to "receive" ideas and information and those have focused on claims of access to government files. In *Leander v. Sweden*, the Court held that the right to receive information under Article 10 "basically prohibits a Government from restricting a person from receiving information that others may wish or may be willing to impart to him." In *Z v. Austria*, Application no. 10392/83, 56 DR 13, admissibility decision of 13 April 1988, the Commission held that freedom to receive information is "primarily a freedom of access to general sources of information which may not be restricted by positive action of the authorities."

While the Convention does not apply to private actions, the Court concluded, however, in one case that an official reprimand by a professional association qualified as a public action. This raises the question of whether a "self-regulatory" code of conduct adopted by an association of ISPs would rise to the level of action covered by the Convention. The answer will depend on a country-by-country understanding of the nature of the association, its relationship with the government, the circumstances under which a particular "code of conduct" was adopted, and the mechanism, if any, for enforcing the code and sanctioning an ISP that did not comply. Given governments' increasing reliance on "self-regulation" to achieve public objectives, a broader interpretation of what constitutes public action may be needed.

Declaration on the Freedom of Expression

European countries also manifested their commitment to free speech in the Council of Europe's 1982 Declaration on the Freedom of Expression and Information ("Council of Europe Declaration"). This Declaration reaffirms Article 10 of the European Convention and proclaims that the freedom of expression is *"a fundamental element [of] the principles of genuine democracy, the rule of law and respect for human rights."* The Declaration also provides that the freedom of expression and information is *"necessary for the social, economic, cultural and political development of every human being, and constitutes a condition for the harmonious progress of social and cultural groups, nations and the international community."* The Council of Europe Declaration thus recognizes that the freedom of expression serves not only an individual interest, but the interests of nation states and the international community as well.

Significant in the context of Internet communication, the Council of Europe Declaration recognizes that *"the continued development of information and communication technology should serve to further that right, regardless of frontiers, to express, seek, to receive and to impart information and ideas, whatever their source."* To achieve this high level of protection, the Council of Europe member states agreed to the following objectives:

— "absence of censorship or any arbitrary controls or constraints on participants in the information process, on media content or on the transmission and dissemination of information;

— "the availability and access on reasonable terms to adequate facilities for the domestic and international transmission and dissemination of information and ideas; [and]

— "to ensure that new information and communication techniques and services, where available, are effectively used to broaden the scope of freedom of expression and information."

New Europe and other OSCE Instruments

The 55-member Organization for Security and Co-operation in Europe ("OSCE"), formerly known as the Conference on Security and Co-operation in Europe, sponsored the 1990 Charter of Paris for a New Europe. Signed by 31 countries from Europe, Russia, Canada, and the United States, the Charter proclaims: *"We affirm that, without discrimination, every individual has the right to freedom of thought, conscience and religion or belief, [and] freedom of expression."*

The OSCE's 1994 Budapest Summit Declaration, "Towards a Genuine Partnership in a New Era," complements the Charter by asserting that participating members *"take as their guiding principle that they will safeguard"* the right to freedom of expression and recognize that *"independent and pluralistic media are essential to a free and open society."* The Internet is the most "independent and pluralistic" of all media; it should therefore benefit from the strongest protection against restrictions on the free flow of information.

OSCE member states also have committed to making *"efforts to facilitate the freer and wider dissemination of information of all kinds [and] to encourage co-operation in the field of information."* In accordance with this commitment, and in recognition of commitments made under the Universal Declaration and the ICCPR, the OSCE declared that its member states *"will ensure that individuals can freely choose their sources of information."*

Finally, countries of the OSCE reaffirmed the ICCPR's limitations on the scope of permissible restrictions on the right of free expression. The 1990 Conference on the Human Dimension concluded that any restrictions on fundamental rights and freedoms must be

1) provided by law;
2) consistent with obligations under international law, particularly those made pursuant to the ICCPR and the Universal Declaration; and
3) must relate to one of the objectives of the applicable law and be strictly proportionate to the aim of that law.

The American Declaration of the Rights and Duties of Convention on Human Rights

Regional agreements from the Americas also explicitly embrace the freedom of expression. The American Declaration of the Rights and Duties of Man was the first international human rights instrument, predating even the Universal Declaration. Article IV of the American Declaration states: *"Every person has the right to freedom of... expression and dissemination of ideas, by any medium whatsoever."*

The American Convention on Human Rights ("American Convention") was adopted in 1969 and entered into force in 1978. It is worth quoting in full, for several of its provisions are of particular relevance to current debates concerning the Internet:

— "Everyone has the right to freedom of thought and expression. This right includes freedom to seek, receive, and impart information and ideas of all kinds, regardless of frontiers, either orally, in writing, in print, in the form of art, or through any other medium of one's choice.

— "The exercise of the right provided for in the foregoing paragraph shall not be subject to prior censorship but shall be subject to subsequent imposition of liability, which shall be expressly established by law to the extent necessary to ensure:

a. respect for the rights or reputations of others; or

b. the protection of national security, public order, or public health or morals.

— "The right of expression may not be restricted by indirect methods or means, such as the abuse of government or private controls over newsprint, radio broadcasting frequencies, or equipment used in the dissemination of information, or by any other means tending to impede the communication and circulation of ideas and opinions.

— "Notwithstanding the provisions of paragraph 2 above, public entertainments may be subject by law to prior censorship for the sole purpose of regulating access to them for the moral protection of childhood and adolescence.

— "Any propaganda for war and any advocacy of national, racial, or religious hatred that constitute incitements to lawless violence or to any other similar action against any person or group of persons on any grounds including those of race, color, religion, language, or national origin shall be considered as offenses punishable by law."

As is the case with the international and European counterparts to these agreements, the plain language of the American Convention is clearly applicable to the Internet.

Notably, the American Convention has several features that go beyond other human rights instruments. For one, the American Convention explicitly states that the exercise of the right of freedom of expression *"shall not be subject to prior censorship."* The rule against prior censorship is also reinforced by Article 14, which provides for a right of reply by anyone inured by inaccurate or offensive statements or ideas disseminated to the general public.

In a provision that may be relevant to the problems posed by Internet "self-regulation," the American Convention applies to private action and makes it clear that the right of expression may not be restricted by indirect methods or means. Article 13(3) provides that the *"right of expression may not be restricted by indirect means, such as the abuse of government or private controls over newsprint, radio broadcasting frequencies, or equipment used in the dissemination of information, or by another means tending to impede the communication and circulation of ideas and opinions."*

The American Convention, in language identical to the ICCPR, sets forth a list of permitted grounds for restriction, a list narrower than that in the European Convention: restrictions on speech must be *"expressly established by law to the extent necessary to ensure [either] [r]espect for the rights or reputation of others... or [t]he protection of national security, public order, or public health or morals."*

Article 11 of the American Convention, like other international agreements, protects the privacy of personal communications: "No one may be the object of arbitrary or abusive interference with his private life, his family, his home, or his correspondence."

Enforcement of the American Convention

The protections of the Convention are enforced by the Inter-American Commission on Human Rights and by the Inter-American Court of Human Rights.

The Commission is an institution of the Organization of the American States. It has the authority to conduct investigations and make recommendations to both the OAS and to Member States. It can "prepare such studies or reports as it considers advisable in the performance of its duties." It can issue advisory opinions to governments. And it is required to take action on petitions by individuals or NGOs and "communications" by Member States.

The Inter-American Court of Human Rights is the principal judicial organ of the inter-American system. Only the Commission and the States Parties have standing before the Court; individuals cannot directly institute proceedings. The Court hears cases of an adjudicatory (or "contentious") nature and also can issue advisory opinions. Proceedings are instituted by the filing of an application either by a State Party or by the Commission. An individual wishing to bring his or her case before the Court must file at the Commission (after exhausting domestic remedies). The Commission then takes the case to the Court

The Inter-American Court has noted that the American Convention is more generous in its guarantee of freedom of expression than the corresponding provisions of both the European Convention and the ICCPR. The Court stated in one case:

"Freedom of expression is a cornerstone upon which the very existence of a democratic society rests. It is indispensable for the formation of public opinion. ... It represents, in short, the means that enable the community, when exercising its options, to be sufficiently informed. Consequently, it can be said that a society that is not well-informed is not a society that is truly free."

One of the leading opinions of the court has to do with the indirect means of controlling freedom of expression, and specifically with a form of self-regulation. The Compulsory Membership case involved a United States citizen who was working in Costa Rica as a journalist without being a member of the Association of Journalists as required by Costa Rican law. He was convicted of the illegal exercise of the profession of journalism in the absence of membership in the Association. The Court said that any restrictions on the freedom of expression must meet four requirements: the existence of previously established grounds for liability; the express and precise definition of these grounds by law; the legitimacy of the ends sought to be achieved; a showing that these grounds are necessary to ensure the ends.

The Court placed considerable emphasis on the requirement of necessity, in terms that have relevance to attempts to censor the Internet. Following the rulings of the ECHR, the Court concluded that necessity implied the existence of "a pressing social need." It was not enough to demonstrate that the regulation was simply useful, reasonable or desirable. The necessity and hence the legality of restrictions "depend upon a showing that the restrictions are required by a compelling governmental interest." Furthermore, the court held that in accordance with the principle of proportionality, the restriction must be "closely tailored to the accomplishment of the legitimate governmental objective necessitating it."

The Court noted that the Inter-American Convention prohibited private controls on the freedom of expression. It indicated that the type of private controls prohibited by the Convention might arise when monopolies or oligopolies instituted practices that restricted speech. The association of journalists was another form of private control, albeit one backed up by a law compelling membership. In defense of the rule, it was argued that compulsory membership was the normal way to organize a profession in order to guarantee adequate standards, thus better serving the community. The Court found this argument unpersuasive. In order to demonstrate that the restriction was necessary, it had to be shown that the same results could not be achieved by less restrictive measures.

The Commission in a 1994 report adopted and reiterated the principles expressed by the court. The Commission proceeding involved "desacato" laws, which criminalized expression that offended, insulted or threatened a public official in the performance of his or her duties. The Commission found that such laws did not serve a legitimate purpose and were not necessary. The Commission also adopted a test similar to the Brandenburg test in the united States, stating that "criminalization of speech can only apply in those exceptional circumstances when there is an obvious and direct threat of lawless violence."

The African Charter on Human and Peoples' Rights

The African Charter on Human and Peoples' Rights ("African Charter"), adopted by 50 countries of the Organization for African Unity, declares in Article 9: *"Every individual shall have the right to receive information . . . [and] to express and disseminate his opinions within the law."* The plain language of this provision clearly establishes that the African Charter protects the full range of modes of communication among people, including communication on the Internet, as well as access to information on the Internet. The African Charter also provides that the parties "have the duty to promote and ensure through teaching, education and publication, the respect of the rights and freedoms contained in the [African Charter] and to see to it that these freedoms and rights as well as corresponding obligations and duties are understood." Finally, the African Charter circumscribes any potential restrictions on the fundamental right to free expression; instead, Article 27 provides that individuals should exercise protected freedoms "with due regard to the rights of others, collective security, morality and common interest." The African Charter also has an enforcement mechanism that hears individual cases.

Opportunities for the Human Rights Community

Undertaking a judicial case in order to advance the cause

of human rights is always a risky business. It requires careful selection of the complainant, the respondent, and the forum. It calls for a clear-eyed weighing of the chances of success. A poorly conceived case can yield an adverse decision that represents a set back for the cause of liberty.

Mindful of these concerns, it is clear that the international human rights instruments offer opportunities to NGOs seeking to challenge governmental regulation of Internet content and access. In some cases, the most promising venues may be under the regional agreements.

Europe: Individuals or other private parties may seek to take their cases before the European Commission and the European Court, after they have exhausted their domestic remedies. Therefore, an NGO concretely affected by a law or practice could bring a case challenging Internet censorship to the Commission and then to the Court. Complaints in the abstract are excluded, however.

The ECHR also allows the submission of amicus briefs. (Amicus briefs are not accepted by the Commission, although with an applicant's consent it is possible to contribute arguments before the Commission as part of an application.) Article 36(2) of the Rules of the Court provide that "The President of the Court may, in the interest of the proper administration of justice, invite... any person concerned who is not the applicant to submit written comments or take part in hearings." The Council of Europe's Explanatory Report notes that the "person concerned" referred to in Article 36(2) may be a natural or legal person. A person wishing to participate should fax a request to the President of the Court as soon as possible after a case has been brought before the court. A number of NGOs (including Amnesty International and Article 19) have filed such briefs before the Court, and the Court in its judgments has explicitly referred to the arguments and information supplied by amici.

Americas: Under the Inter-American system, while individuals do not have standing to bring their cases directly before the court, they can ask the Commission to take up their cases. Indeed, according to Article 44 of the Inter-American Convention, petitions containing denunciations or complaints of violations of the convention by a State Party may be lodged at the Commission by any person, any group of persons, and any non-governmental organization legally recognized in one or more Member States of the OAS. These categories of potential complainants with standing are considerably broader than those in most other international human rights instruments. There is no requirement that petitioners be the actual victims of a Convention violation. "Furthermore, there is no requirement that the complainant be within the jurisdiction of the respondent state. ... The reference to [NGOs] clearly recognizes the important role which they may discharge in the protection of human rights. ... It should be noted that it matters not that an NGO be legally present and recognized in the territory of the respondent State Party; it is enough that it is recognized in one or more OAS Member States."

United Nations: In preparing its annual reports, the UN's Commission on Human Rights regularly draws on information provided by NGOs. Likewise, the Human Rights Committee, which oversees compliance with the ICCPR through the reporting mechanism, also accepts submissions from NGOs. Both the Commission and the

Committee should be educated on, and urged to examine, Internet issues.

National Laws Restricting Freedom of Expression on the Internet

In the past, it was assumed that a country could control content within its borders, subject to free expression principles, and that publishers had some ability to control and direct the distribution of their materials. (Even in the broadcast realm, there were limits to the reach of most transmitters. But satellite transmission of television signals is forcing a parallel breakdown of borders in the broadcast field.) Thus, in *Handyside,* even though the book at issue was legal in most countries of Europe, Article 10 of the European Convention was not violated by the UK's efforts to prohibit its sale in the UK. If a restriction was justified in a particular country, then it applied to both domestically produced and foreign produced material, even if the foreign material was legal where produced. A magazine printed legally in the Netherlands would have to be tested by German standards if someone wanted to distribute or possess it in Germany.

But this margin of appreciation doctrine — clearly in tension with the language "regardless of frontiers" — was based in large part on the physical nature of the media by which information and ideas were produced and disseminated. Respect for differing legal norms — even though freedom of expression was raised to the level of an international right — was based on the premise that a country had a reasonable chance of success in keeping material out of its territory, at least things like books or reels of film or paintings on canvas, and that publishers had a reasonable chance of success in controlling distribution of their materials.

On the Internet, neither governments nor publishers have this type of control over information, for information is no longer tied to physical objects. The global nature of the Internet should give new relevance to the concept "regardless of frontiers" found in human rights instruments. As Judge Martens said in a separate opinion in the Spycatcher case, "in this 'age of information' information and ideas cannot be stopped at frontiers any longer." Judges Pettiti and Farinha made the same point in their separate opinion: "In the era of satellite television it is impossible territorially to partition thought and its expression or to restrict the right of information of the inhabitants of a country whose newspapers are subject to a prohibition."

Under human rights principles, expression on the Internet will still be subject to restriction, but without the "margin of appreciation" that has supported restrictions in so many cases. The Internet requires the adoption of a true international standard of review, one that must look to consensus rules generally.

The rise of the Internet also requires a reexamination of the meaning of the concept to "seek and receive" and to "impart" information. National restrictions on local speech have a direct and negative impact on the ability of Internet users around the world to "seek and receive" information and ideas, as well as their right to "impart" information. For example, if citizens of one country are prohibited from discussing political issues critically online, then not only are their rights infringed upon, but also the right of others around the world to "seek and receive" that information is directly implicated. Similarly, a country's efforts to block certain content from outside its border implicates the right of those in other countries to "impart" the information. A new rule is called for: only that content can be prohibited which all (or virtually all) countries agree is prohibited.

Indirect Methods of Control are just as Dangerous as Direct Government Censorship

Internet Service Providers (ISPs) play a special role in the operation of the Internet. While ISPs differ in nature from country to country, most people most of the time access the Internet through an ISP. The crucial role ISPs play in providing access to the Internet has made them the target of some governments' efforts to regulate content on the Internet. Those countries have assumed that if they can control ISPs, they can control content on the Internet.

ISPs do not fit any of the existing media paradigms. They are very distinct from broadcasters. For this reason, it is not legitimate to subject them to regulatory structures designed for other technologies.

There are two sets of arguments against making ISPs responsible for content they do not create. First, trying to make ISPs responsible for information that flows over their systems (but which they did not create) would fundamentally change the nature of the Internet and could destroy its power. Second, there is growing recognition that ISPs cannot technically assume responsibility for content they did not create. The task of sifting information is impossible. It would be so easy to encrypt content, to change addresses, to send images by email.

Technical factors prevent a service provider from blocking the free flow of information on the Internet. First, an Internet service provider cannot easily stop the incoming flow of material. No one can monitor the enormous quantity of network traffic, which may consist of hundreds of thousands of emails, newsgroup messages, files, and Web pages that pass through in dozens of text and binary formats, some of them readable only by particular proprietary tools. As the European Commission noted recently, "it is as yet unclear how far it is technically possible to block access to content once it is identified as illegal."

A second technical problem is that a provider cannot selectively disable transmission to particular users. Electronic networks typically do not allow for the identification of particular users or their national region. ISPs cannot provide material in one country while blocking it in another; such a distinction would require an enormous new infrastructure on top of the current network. Some networking technologies, such as newsgroups, may allow individual operators to select some groups or items and block others. But many technologies, such as the World Wide Web, currently do not support such selectivity.

A number of countries have recognized, after considerable study and debate, that ISPs should not be liable for content they did not create. This reflects a judgment that while ISPs ought to provide law enforcement reasonable assistance in investigating criminal activity, confusing the role of private companies and police authorities risks substantial violation of individual civil liberties. In 1997, Germany adopted a Multimedia Law (the Information and Communications Services Act) which provides that access providers are not responsible for any third-party content to which they only provide access. Providers also are not responsible for "any third-party content which they make available for use unless they have knowledge of such content and are technically able and can reasonably be expected to block the use of such content."

In the United States, section 230 of the Communications Act, 47 United States Code sec.230, states "No Provider or user of an interactive computer service shall be treated as the publisher or speaker of any information provided by another information content provider." In adopting this provision, Congress specifically found that "the Internet and other interactive computer services offer a forum for a true diversity of political discourse, unique opportunities for cultural development, and myriad avenues for intellectual activity," and it said that its goal was "to promote the continued development of the Internet."

The European Commission also has concluded that regulation of ISPs was not the best way to address content regulation. In its 1996 Communication to the European Parliament, The Council, The Economic and Social Committee and the Committee of the Regions on Illegal and Harmful Content on the Internet, the Commission stated that "Internet access providers and host service providers play a key role in giving users access to Internet content. It should not however be forgotten that the prime responsibility for content lies with authors and content providers."

The Commission stated that blocking access at the level of access providers would go far beyond the limited category of illegal content and "such a restrictive regime is inconceivable for Europe as it would severely interfere with the freedom of the individual and its political traditions." Therefore "the law may need to be changed or clarified to assist access providers and host service providers, whose primary business is to provide a service to customers."

"Therefore, the position of the ISPs should be clarified, and they should not be targeted by the individual governments and law enforcement bodies where the ISPs have no control of the Internet content." The European Parliament in its decision of 13 May 1998 and the Council of The European Union in it recommendation of 28 May 1998 both agreed with the Commission and concluded, in effect, that ISPs should not be liable for content they did not create.

The "Bonn Declaration" of European Ministers likewise underlined the importance of clearly defining the relevant legal rules on responsibility for content of the various actors in the chain between creation and use. The Declaration recognized the need to make a clear distinction between the responsibility of those who produce and place content in circulation and that of intermediaries such as the Internet Service Providers.

In the EU and in a number of other countries, "self-regulation" has been offered as a viable alternative to governmental control of Internet content. The use of the term "self-regulation" is a misnomer in the context of controlling speech on the Internet. In the normal sense of the phrase, "self-regulation" is when a group of people or companies decide that, in their own best interest, they should themselves regulate how they go about their joint interests. However, what is being suggested by the term "self-regulation" as applied to the Internet is not that ISPs as a group should regulate their own behavior, but rather that ISPs should regulate the behavior of their customers by taking down offensive websites or blocking offensive content.

Under international law, privatized control may be harder to challenge. However, in a number of cases, it may be clear that the ISP is acting under pressure from the government and has, in essence become the agent of the government for carrying out a government policy. What is often promoted as Internet "self-regulation" is actually "privatized censorship." It is consistent with the fairly common occurrence of having a formerly direct government function turned over to a private business. The backing is still state power and government threat, but the actual implementation and mechanics of the suppression of material is delegated to a trade group.

GILC member Cyber-Rights & Cyber-Liberties (UK) wrote in its report "Who Watches the Watchmen: Internet Content Rating Systems, and Privatised Censorship"

"The current situation at the UK does not represent a self-regulatory solution as suggested by the UK Government. It is moving towards a form of censorship, a privatised and industry based one where there will be no space for dissent as it will be done by the use of private organisations, rating systems and at the entry level by putting pressure on the UK Internet Service Providers. One can only recall the events which took place in the summer of 1996 and how the ISPs were pressured by the Metropolitan police to remove around 130 newsgroups from their servers."

If it can be shown that "self-regulatory" measures are mere proxies for more direct government control, they may be vulnerable to challenge under human rights law. For one, they do not meet the test of proportionality. When ISPs come together to self-regulate certain classes of content in exchange for some limit on their liability for that content, the overwhelming tendency will be to censor more material, rather than less, in an effort by the ISPs to be certain that they have removed any material that might be illegal. Where ISPs are dependent on government grants of liability limitations, their "self-regulating" actions must satisfy the perceived demands of law enforcement, even if this results in removal of legal, protected speech.

Initial reports from "self-regulatory" systems cast doubt on their effectiveness and suggest that the only effective way to combat crime such as child pornography is with well trained police. The two most important hotlines in Europe, the Dutch hotline and the UK hotline, have observed that despite the large amount of complaints they receive, this amount is tiny compared to the vast volume available on the Internet. The effects these hotlines have on dissemination of illegal content is also tiny. The Dutch Hotline, in its annual report, warned that it had absolutely no effect on distribution of illegal content in chat-boxes and E-mail, and that its influence on such distribution in newsgroups was very limited. According to the Internet Watch Foundation Annual Report, of the 4,300 items blocked by private action, "[o]nly the few articles appearing to have originated in the UK are suitable for investigation and action by the UK police." Thus with little measurable law enforcement impact, thousands of presumably legal items were nevertheless removed from the Internet.

Blocking, filtering, and labeling techniques can restrict freedom of expression and limit access to information when used or mandated by governments or their agents. Specifically, such techniques can prevent individuals from using the Internet to exchange information on topics that may be controversial or unpopular, enable the development of country profiles to facilitate a global/universal rating system desired by governments, block access to content on entire domains, block access to Internet content available at any domain or page which contains a specific key-word or character string in the URL, and over-ride self-rating labels provided by content creators and providers.

Government-mandated use of blocking, filtering, and labeling systems are subject to the same limitations under basic international human rights protections as other Internet restrictions: No matter what the means, government restriction on speech or access to speech of others violates basic freedom of expression protections. Filtering is inappropriate in public educational institutions and libraries.

In its statement to the OECD in March 1998, GILC articulated several policy principles related to filtering and labeling:

Global rating or labeling systems squelch the free flow of information: Efforts to force all Internet speech to be labeled or rated according to a single classification system will distort the fundamental cultural diversity of the Internet and will lead to domination of one set of political or moral viewpoints. Such systems will either be easy to use and not have enough categories for all cultures or they will have so many categories to cater to all cultures that they will be unusable. These systems are antithetical to the Internet and should be rejected.

Infrastructure distortions to force labeling must be rejected: Extra-legal means of forcing individuals to use filtering, labels or ratings such as ratings requirements in search engines or default settings in browsers restrict the free flow of information online and distort the basic openness of the Internet.

Transparency must be maintained: Users must be made aware if their Internet access is being filtered, and, if so, based on what filtering system. They must also be able to disable the filtering at any point.

White lists are preferable to black lists: Access to a variety of tools which make positive suggestions (white lists), pointing to certain content, rather than blocking content (black lists), should be encouraged.

Diversity is essential: To the extent that individuals choose to employ filtering tools, it is vital that they have access to a wide variety of such tools.

An Important Guarantor of Free Expression

Central to free expression and the protection of privacy is the right to express political beliefs without fear of retribution and to control the disclosure of personal identity. Protecting the right of anonymity is therefore an essential goal for the protection of personal freedoms in the online world.

Anonymity has been an integral part of the growth and development of the Internet. Some governments are working to extend techniques for anonymity. The Netherlands and the Canadian province of Ontario are pursuing studies on anonymity. The German government has recently adopted legislation that would encourage the adoption of anonymous payments systems for the Internet.

But other efforts are underway to establish mandatory identification requirements and to limit the use of techniques that protect anonymity. For example, in December 1997, the Interior and Justice Ministers of the G-8 endorsed a proposal to require identification for Internet users. Some governments have also tried adopt legislation that would prohibit access to the Internet without the disclosure of personal identity.

Governments should not require the identification of Internet users or restrict the ability to express political beliefs on the Internet anonymously. Efforts to develop new techniques to protect anonymity and identity should be encouraged. The governments of Canada, Germany, and the Netherlands are to be commended for their recent efforts to support anonymity. ISPs should not establish unnecessary identification requirements for customers and should, wherever practicable, preserve the right of users to access the Internet anonymously.

The vast majority of Internet use is for legitimate and indeed positive purposes. The effect of access and use of this global interactive medium has been to promote democracy and civil society worldwide. On the Internet, citizens are not mere consumers of content but also creators of content.

The Internet is a unique communication medium. It is more than a mere industry. Like no other medium before, it allows individuals to express their ideas and opinions directly to a world audience, while allowing them access to other ideas, opinions and information to which they may not otherwise have access.

While the mass media usually responds to the economic and political interests of those who control it, such controls do not presently exist on the Internet. Here, citizens from the most repressive regimes are able to find information about matters concerning their governments or their human rights records that no local newspaper may dare print, while denouncing the conditions under which they live for the world to hear. The Internet allows us an intimate look at other countries, other people and other cultures which few before were ever able to attain. This power to give and receive information, so central to any conception of democracy, can be truly achieved on the Internet, as nowhere before.

Restrictions on the free flow of information on the Internet should be subject to the strongest protections under international law. The free flow of information and ideas is the very essence of the Internet. One state's restrictions on Internet content infringe upon the rights of all Internet users around the world to benefit from a free exchange of social, political, economic, cultural, scientific, and personal information.

Technology surely will outpace states' efforts to restrict the free flow of information on the Internet. New methods of accessing the Internet, for example by satellite, will make territorial boundaries even less relevant to the Internet than they are today. Attempts to suppress information and communication on the Internet, therefore, not only violate international human rights laws, in the end they are likely to be futile.

7

Internet Policy Principles

The Internet is an inherently open, decentralized communications infrastructure which is ideally suited to support the free exchange of ideas, a rich political discourse, and a vibrant economy. The decentralized architecture of the Internet provides an abundance of communication opportunities, and gives users an unprecedented degree of control over the information that they receive. As organizations devoted to basic human rights, the growth of the Internet, and the flourishing of democratic culture, we believe that the foregoing principles will ensure that the Internet remains open and continues to support basic democratic values.

Policymaking and the Internet

In recognition of the novel and rapidly changing nature of the Internet, policymaking ought to be undertaken:

— policymakers who are well informed about the unique nature of the Internet and have direct experience with its use; and,

— With substantial input and comment from the Internet user community.

Internet Access and Market Structures

Access to the global Internet and other interactive communications infrastructures is essential for all citizens of the world to enable full participation in the global society and developing digital economy. Government and the industry have a shared responsibility in building the Global Information Infrastructure ("GII"), and in ensuring as wide an access as possible to its services.

Competition, open systems and interoperability are the best way to enlarge access. In particular, access to the Internet by schools, libraries and other public institutions should be viewed as a policy goal, subsidized as necessary.

Access to Government Information

Governments should enable citizens access to legislative, judicial and executive branch information through the Internet. Such access should be backed up by a legal right to public information, without any showing of need or intended use. Such information should be available in standard formats to promote broad and effective access.

Market structures

There should be no a priori limitation to market entry for Internet service providers (ISPs), and ISPs should not be prevented from using or establishing their own terrestrial or wireless infrastructure.

In particular, licensing should not be used as a method of restricting market entry. ISPs and other intermediaries have responsibilities, but those responsibilities should be enforced other than through licensing mechanisms.

Overseas Development Assistance

Overseas development assistance programs should strive to promote full access to the Internet. Such programs should include support for the development of public policy environments consistent with these Open Internet Policy Principles, and adequate resources for training and ongoing support.

Rights and Responsibilities of Internet Users

Internet users have rights and responsibilities which should shape the way the law addresses the Internet.

General legal framework

The Internet does not exist in a legal vacuum. For the most part, existing laws can and should regulate conduct on the Internet to the same degree as other forms of conduct. Such laws may differ from country to country, but should conform with the applicable binding human rights obligations contained in the Universal Declaration of Human Rights, the International Covenant on Civil and Political Rights and the European Convention on Human Rights.

The legality of publishing activity on the Internet should be judged according to the law in the country in which the publisher originally acts to publish the material. While this "law of the place of origin" is consistent with the "Television Without Borders" policy of the European Commission, strong public policies in places of reception may necessitate negotiation of an international convention on this choice-of-law question.

Objectionable content

To enable users to shield themselves and their families from objectionable or unwanted content, priority should be given to "downstream filtering" by users. There should be no government censorship of Internet content.

Filtering should empower users to be responsible for the content they access.

Filtering can promote freedom of choice through a variety of rating systems.

Filtering systems should make clear what sites they block (or select) and what criteria they use to block (or select) sites.

Access to multiple 3rd party content labeling systems, as opposed to government censorship, can support the great diversity of cultural and moral values of Internet users around the world.

Law, Human Rights and the Internet

Legal regulation of the Internet should implement the foregoing principles relating to rights and responsibilities of Internet users, while also recognizing international human rights law and legitimate national law enforcement interests.

Freedom of Expression

There should be no regulation of Internet content by government. We understand the fundamental rights of freedom of expression, as embodied in Art. 19 of the Universal Declaration of Human Rights ("Everybody has the right ... to seek, receive and impart information and ideas through any media and regardless of frontiers") and in Art. 19(2) of the International Covenant on Civil and Political Rights ("Everyone shall have the right to freedom of expression; this right shall include freedom to seek, receive and impart information and ideas of all kinds, regardless of frontiers, either orally, in writing or in print, in the form or art or through any other media of his choice") — to apply with full force to Internet communication.

Civil and criminal law enforcement

Enforcing existing laws in the international Internet environment raises specific challenges. In general,combating online crime, while protecting civil liberties, can best be accomplished with additional resources and training for law enforcement agencies, not by enactment of new laws.

In carrying out their duties, law enforcement agencies should:

— Be fully aware of the unique characteristics of the Internet;

— Adhere to internationally recognized principles of human rights;

— Have the resources necessary to adopt appropriate technologies; and

— Co-ordinate with other law enforcement agencies across international boundaries.

Law enforcement activity should be guided by the following principles:

— Law enforcement agents should only conduct investigations or surveillance in public online fora pursuant to public and officially approved investigative guidelines, which provide adequate protection for individual freedom of association and political activity.

— Governments should not monitor individual Internet users for civil or criminal investigatory purposes nor collect information on the way they use the Internet, except pursuant to a judicial process that is consistent with internationally recognized principles of privacy.

— Governmental searches or seizure of electronic communications should not be conducted, except pursuant to legally authorized procedures, that require that there is sufficient evidence that the user is engaged in illegal activity to justify the search. Any such search should be supervised by an appropriate detached and neutral judicial officer. Any search should be narrow in its scope and effect.

Communications privacy

Users of the Internet should have the right to be free of unlawful governmental interception of or access to communication and information online. Protection of this right entails:

Right of Anonymity: Users should have the right to communicate without disclosing their identity. Anonymous communication is critical to assure basic rights of freedom of association and to protect an open political process. By the same token, anonymous communication is not traceable by law enforcement. Thus, we recognize that some criminal investigations may be made more difficult. As the Internet develops, we believe that some services will develop that support anonymous speech, while others will require identification. Choice among various levels of identification should be made by the users involved, not dictated by law.

Unfettered Right to Use Encryption: Users should have the right to use any form of cryptographic technology they choose to protect the privacy of their communications. Users should not be compelled to guarantee in advance law enforcement access to communications through key escrow, key recovery or other mechanisms.

Freedom from Unlawful Access to Information in Storage or Transmission: No user should be subjected to governmental search or seizure of electronic communications except pursuant to legally authorized procedures, supervised by an appropriate detached and neutral judicial officer.

Users should have better notice and choice over the use of personal information by others. User empowerment approaches can also address these information privacy issues in interactive system environments.

When there was a difference of opinion among conference participants as to a particular Principle, a vote was taken, with the majority view prevailing. All conference participants agreed that views not prevailing would be included in an Annex to the Final Document.

There was a majority vote by conference participants in favor of removing the following draft Principle from the Final Document:

Responsibility for content on the Internet should rest with the author of the content. It is crucial to identify accurately the chain of responsibilities. Originators of content should be responsible for the content they put on the Internet - not access providers, network operators, storage facilities or other intermediaries. When anonymity makes it impossible to fix responsibility on the author or originator, responsibility should rest with the last first identifiable individual or entity in the chain of distribution, closest to the author or originator, who had an opportunity to accept or decline anonymous material.

Professor Hank Perritt of Villanova University Law School has provided the following opinion in support of the draft Principle above that was removed from the Final Document:

There is a tension between protecting anonymity and protecting intermediaries from liability. The best rule would be to protect intermediaries from liability as long as it is possible to identify the originator or author of a communication. If an intermediary handles anonymous communications, however, the only choice is to let a victim of a harmful communication bear the loss or to shift the loss to the intermediary. As between the innocent victim, who has no choice, and the intermediary who has a choice whether to accept anonymous communication, it would be preferable to hold the intermediary liable. Accordingly, we would favor an immunity for intermediaries but only as to non-anonymous messages or other items of information content.

Two conference participants,Christopher Kuner, Attorney-at-Law, Gleiss & Partners, Germany (on behalf of Netscape Communications Corporation) and Professor Hank Perritt of Villanova University Law School, have expressed reservations about Principle III(A)2 in the Final Document:

Christopher Kuner: Principle III(A)(2) is unclear, legally questionable, and does not reflect our discussion at the conference. In particular, I would like to point out the following:

— The wording of this principle is unclear; just what is "the country in which the publisher originally acts to publish the material" when, for instance, an Internet user transmits material he has authored to a server in another country, from which it can be accessed over the net?

— The principle is inconsistent with the rest of the draft. Under this language, the conduct of someone sitting at a computer in Iran who publishes a web page saying "Khomeini was a liar and a crook" should be judged based on Iranian law, whereas in Article III(A)(1) we talk about "binding human rights obligations" and in Article IV about "international human rights law", both of which would likely be violated by the sanctions which Iranian law would impose on such a person.

— Why does it matter whether or not a document concerned with the Internet is consistent with EU television policy?

— The law of most countries and international law provide for the possibility of law being applied to conduct outside the borders of the jurisdiction which enacted it when such conduct produces a harmful effect in the jurisdiction. I may not always agree with this approach, but find that Article III(A)(2) simply glosses over this principle without explaining why it should not apply in the case of the Internet.

— The choice of law provision embodied in Article III(A)(2) was mentioned in the closing minutes of the conference as an afterthought, and we never had a chance to discuss it. The subject of choice of law in the Internet is extremely complex, and I object to taking a position on it when we never had a chance to consider it properly.

Professor Hank Perritt: Choice of law is tricky in Cyberspace. International law arguably permits both the country of origin to regulate content on the Internet. There is precedent for both approaches. The "Television Without Borders" document from the EC adopts the country-of-origin approach, making content legal anywhere if it is legal in the country of origin and presumably illegal anywhere if it is illegal in the country of origin. The UN General Assembly resolution on direct broadcast television adopts the country of receipt approach, making the content legal if it is legal in the country of receipt, and presumably illegal according to the local law of the place of receipt as well.

Neither of these approaches is perfect. In the long run, it would be better to harmonize content rules, and efforts should begin now to narrow differences on content regulation, recognizing a general preference in favor of freedom of expression, as noted in the principles.

8

Cybercensorship

The Internet offers protean possibilities for evading controls on the flow of information. In countries where there is no local ISP, persons can, for the price of an international call, dial service providers in other countries. If a web site is blocked, its sponsors or fans can change its address or "mirror" the same content at other World Wide Web sites. Local users can view web sites that are blocked by accessing them via free "anti-censorship proxy (ACP) servers." They can also have persons who enjoy access to content that is blocked locally e-mail it to them as attached files. Wary e-mail correspondents can foil surveillance by using pseudonymous e-mail accounts or encryption, or by routing messages through a Web-based re-mailing service that "anonymizes" them by stripping information that identifies the sender.

But if the tricks available to users are bountiful, so is the technology on the other side of the cat-and-mouse game. Governments may not be able to stop, but they can certainly slow the flow of "objectionable" content and thus buy time to adjust to an era in which their ability to block or crowd out information is diminished.

State's can deny the public local access to the Internet altogether, as Iraq, Libya, Syria and, until recently Saudi Arabia have done. But neither Syria nor Saudi Arabia has gone so far as to prohibit possession of modems or connections to foreign Internet providers. Both Riyadh and Damascus have thus tolerated a limited and gradually increasing amount of Internet access rather than adopt the draconian measures required to prevent access to foreign ISPs, which would likely antagonize the members of the public wealthy enough to afford it.

Governments that presently allow public local access to the Internet have adopted a range of methods to regulate that access. The Global Internet Liberty Campaign divides these methods into four categories: Internet-specific laws; application of existing laws; content-based license (or contract) terms applied to users and service providers, and compulsory use of filtering, rating or content labeling tools. All of these methods can be found in the Middle East and North Africa, along with extra-legal measures that also diminish online freedoms.

Laws and licensing terms: Tunisia has developed the region's most detailed Internet-specific laws. Tunisia also explicitly extends to the Internet existing press laws limiting free expression, something that few other countries in the region have done. However, the existing press laws of several countries, in their delineation of offenses, define "publishing" or "disseminating" information in so broad a fashion that no new laws are needed to bring Internet speech under their purview. Qatari Internet users must sign a contract with the Qatar Public Telecommunications Corporation pledging not to use the service to "carry out any activity which is contrary to public order". Asked for the definition of this phrase, Qatar's embassy in Washington replied that while there is no "concise definite context of the phrase," it "refers in general to the necessity of commitment to the State's public policies and to the community's traditions and values."

Filtering of content: The United Arab Emirates has set up a "proxy server" that denies user access to sites deemed inappropriate, mostly because of their explicit sexuality. Bahrain, Iran, Yemen, Tunisia, and Saudi Arabia also block web sites, using a variety of technical means available to filter and block content. Blocking is easier to implement for governments that retain control over the national telecommunications network, including the international gateways. Nearly everywhere in the region, telecommunications remain a state-controlled monopoly. And even in the few countries that have allowed some privatization of Internet services, such as Egypt, the international gateway remains under state control.

In addition to technical and legal means, other government practices, including threats and intimidation, can create a chilling effect on online speech, just as such practices often do more than press laws to constrain what private newspapers and magazines are willing to print. Fears of government surveillance or reprisals, for example, can foster self-censorship in a newspaper, a web site, or an online "chat room." In Jordan, for example, at least two persons were reportedly summoned for questioning by the police during 1996 because of articles or comments they had posted on electronic bulletin boards or in chat rooms--forums whose contents can be read by everyone, including the police.

No government in the region, to our knowledge, has admitted to "eavesdropping" on e-mail, and Human Rights Watch has no proof that it is taking place. Yet given the technical ease of conducting this sort of surveillance--especially when all Internet access goes through a gateway that is maintained by a state-controlled institution-- and the fact that police forces in so many countries of the region tap the phones and open the mail of real and suspected dissidents, it is not surprising to hear fears expressed by Internet users in Tunisia, Bahrain, and other countries about the privacy of their electronic communications.

Authorities monitor telephone conversations in at least thirteen countries of the region, according to the U.S. Department of State's Country Reports on Human Rights Practices for 1998, and in most they did so without legally issued warrants or judicial supervision. Those who suspect online surveillance often cite instances of e-mails inexplicably disappearing en route or taking two days to reach their destination. Such occurrences can be caused by snooping but of course may have other explanations as well.

9

Silencing the Net: Threat to On-Line

This chapter the evolving policies of governments in the Middle East and North Africa affecting the right of persons to receive and impart information through the Internet. It aims to reinforce and expand online freedoms not only by identifying violations of free expression rights that have taken place, but also by proposing--at a time when Internet laws and policies are being developed--steps governments should take to protect and enhance the rights of all persons to exchange information and ideas freely through this medium.

In a region where torture is commonplace and free elections the exception, the issue of Internet speech may seem low on the human rights agenda. It may also appear to be an elitist concern in countries where illiteracy is rampant and the cost of a personal computer and perhaps even a telephone is beyond the reach of most households.

But it is arguably in less-developed and in more repressive countries that the Internet can have the greatest impact. Wherever it is accessible, the Internet has provided dramatic new possibilities for people to obtain and exchange information locally and internationally. It has been hailed by many as a force for eroding authoritarian political control and aiding participatory democracy.

As the first truly "mass" medium, one that is inherently open and decentralized, the Internet can enable anyone to receive and to disseminate alternatives to state-controlled information at a low cost. While few individuals and groups have the means to publish books or newspapers, make a film, or air a radio or television program, any person with access to a personal computer and modem can communicate with a huge international audience. A connection to the Internet can increase access to information in less-developed countries by putting within easy reach one of the world's great repositories of information, much of it free and continuously updated, and by making that information more easily manageable and transferable.

Such benefits do not depend on a large number of persons having the means to purchase their own equipment and Internet accounts. A government policy of making computers available to the public at libraries, schools or community centers, or the presence of privately run "Internet cafés" or "cybercafés" (shops offering the public fee-for-use Internet access), can help to democratize use of the Internet even in relatively poor countries.

In light of the Internet's vast potential for empowering people to exercise the right to free expression, some have argued that governments have an affirmative obligation to facilitate Internet access for all segments of the population on terms of nondiscrimination. Some have also contended that the Internet can significantly assist governments in enabling citizens to exercise the right, under article 25(a) of the International Covenant on Civil and Political Rights, "to take part in the conduct of public affairs, directly or through freely chosen representatives." The exercise of this right is enhanced by providing citizens access to all draft and effective laws, transcripts of parliamentary debates, and other information relevant to civic affairs. As the Global Internet Liberty Campaign (GILC) notes, "In almost every country in the world, most government information is now created by word processing, meaning that the information is already digitized...[and] can be rapidly and inexpensively put on-line, even using simple Gopher technology."

The Internet's potential contribution to democratic and participatory politics is gaining recognition. In his 1998 report to the U.N. Commission on Human Rights, the Special Rapporteur on the promotion and protection of the right to freedom of opinion and expression outlined the case against government regulation of Internet access and content as follows:

The new technologies and, in particular, the Internet, are inherently democratic, provide the public and individuals with access to information and sources and enable all to participate actively in the communication process. The Special Rapporteur also believes that action by States to impose excessive regulations on the use of these technologies and, again, particularly the Internet, on the grounds that control, regulation and denial of access are necessary to preserve the moral fabric and cultural identity of societies is paternalistic. These regulations presume to protect people from themselves and, as such are inherently incompatible with the principles of the worth and dignity of each individual.

Internet connectivity is of special significance to civil society. Computer networks fill a "media gap" between interpersonal communication facilitated by telephone, telegram, and letters, and mass communication facilitated by radio, television, and print media. Computer networks can greatly facilitate small-group participation--within groups, between groups, and between groups and their constituencies--and thus help to strengthen the forces of civil society. Many human rights organizations have embraced the Internet as a means of exchanging information quickly and cheaply. Groups in the Middle East and North Africa have proved no exception to this trend.

Governments around the world, claiming they want to protect children,thwart terrorists and silence racists and hate mongers, are rushing toeradicate freedom of expression on the Internet, the international "network ofnetworks," touted as the Information Superhighway. It is particularly crucialnow, in the early stages of vast technological change, that governmentsreaffirm their commitment to respect the rights of citizens to communicatefreely. A G7 Ministerial Conference on the Information Society and Developmentto be held in South Africa from May 13-15, 1996 should be used as a platformto repudiate the international trend toward censorship and to expressunequivocal support for free expression guarantees on-line.

Restrictions on Internet access and content are increasing worldwide,under all forms of government.

Censorship legislation was recently enacted inthe United States, the birthplace of the Bill of Rights as well as of this newcommunications medium and, for better or worse, a model for other nations'Internet policies. The Clinton administration claims the law will protectminors from "indecent" material and appears unconcerned that it will reduceon-line expression between adults to what may be deemed suitable for a child.Other democratic countries are following suit. The German phone company cutoff access to all the sites hosted by an American Internet service provider(ISP) in an effort to bar Germans from gaining access to neo-Nazi propagandaon one of the sites it hosted. The governments of France and Australia havealso indicated they may enact legislation to control Internet content.

Authoritarian regimes are attempting to reconcile their eagerness to reap the economic benefits of Internet access with maintaining control over the flow of information inside their borders. Censorship efforts in the U.S. and Germany lend support to those in China, Singapore, and Iran, where censors target not only sexually explicit material and hate speech but also pro-democracy discussions and human rights education.

Proposals to censor the Internet wherever they originate violate the free speech guarantees enshrined in democratic constitutions and international law. In the attempt to enforce them, open societies will become increasingly repressive and closed societies will find new opportunity to chill political expression.

Because the Internet knows no national boundaries, on-line censorship laws, in addition to trampling on the free expression rights of a nation's own citizens, threaten to chill expression globally and to impede the development of the Global Information Infrastructure (GII) before it becomes a truly global phenomenon. Democratic countries, including the U.S. and Germany, that are pushing for the development of the GII will lack legitimacy in criticizing efforts by China to eliminate information that "hinders public order" or by

Vietnam, where the "the cultural aspect" is cited as a reason to censor connections to pro-democracy discussions abroad. (According to Nghiem Yuan Tinh, deputy director of Vietnam Data Communication Company, "The Internet must be controlled, not only for technical and security reasons but from the cultural aspect." "Plan by Telecom Authority to Exercise Control Over Internet Disturbs Foreign Investors and Agency," Financial Times (London).

An issue closely related to censorship is that of access, which is to a large extent determined by the existing telecommunications system. According to a 1995 report by the Panos Institute, a London-based international non-profit organization specializing in development issues,

Access requires a telephone line. Forty-nine countries have fewer than one telephone per 100 people, 35 of which are in Africa. India, for example, has 8 million telephone lines for 900 million people. At a global level at least 80% of the world's population still lacks the most basic telecommunications. (The Internet and the South: Superhighway or Dirt-Track?

Opportunities to promote access have never been greater, however. New communications technologies are providing developing countries with an unprecedented means to leapfrog antiquated communication networks.

Limits on access are imposed by governments for a variety of reasons, including economic gain and political control. Some governments, including India and Saudi Arabia, have chosen to control the liberalizing effect of the Internet by denying access to entire segments of their populations, either through exorbitant charges or by confining access to select populations, such as universities. Rather than attempting to extend the Internet to a diverse group of citizens, these governments are striving to reap the economic benefits of Internet access without making it available to economically, socially, and politically disadvantaged groups, for whom it has the greatest potential for positive change. In some countries, such as Saudi Arabia, individuals who have Internet connections through foreign-owned corporations are able to elude these restrictions.

Even at this relatively early stage in the Internet's development, a wide range of restrictions on on-line communication have been put in place in at least twenty countries, including the following:

— China, which requires users and Internet Service Providers (ISPs) to register with authorities;

— Vietnam and Saudi Arabia, which permit only a single, government- controlled gateway for Internet service;

— United States, which has enacted new Internet-specific legislation that imposes more restrictive regulations on electronic expression than those currently applied to printed expression;

— India, which charges exorbitant rates for international access through the state-owned phone company;

— Germany, which has cut off access to particular host computers or Internet sites;

— Singapore, which has chosen to regulate the Internet as if it were a broadcast medium, and requires political and religious content providers to register with the state; and

— New Zealand, which classifies computer disks as publications and has seized and restricted them accordingly.

Privacy issues are closely related to the regulation of content and access. On-line communications are particularly susceptible to unauthorized scrutiny. Encryption technology is needed to ensure that individuals and groups may communicate without fear of eavesdropping. Lack of information privacy will inhibit on-line speech and unnecessarily limit the diversity of voices on the GII.

The Internet has the potential to be a tremendous force for development by providing quick and inexpensive information, by encouraging discussion rather than violence, and by empowering citizens, to cite but a few examples.

But this potential can be realized only if it becomes a truly global effort. Policy makers must make every effort to ensure that internationally guaranteed rights to free expression are extended to on-line communication and call for the repeal of censorship legislation. Without such commitments, individuals face the danger of seeing their rights eroded by the very technologies they are embracing.

This report recommends principles for international and regional bodies and nations to follow when formulating public policy and laws affecting the Internet, sets forth the international legal principles governing on-line expression, and, finally, examines some of the current attempts around the globe to censor on-line communication.

RECOMMENDATIONS

The meeting of the G7 countries (Britain, Canada, France, Germany, Italy, Japan, and the United States) in South Africa in May 1996 to discuss the development of the GII should be used as one platform to emphasize the importance of freedom of expression.3 (A UNESCO meeting was held in Madrid in March 1996 to discuss copyright protection on the Internet. To our knowledge, that conference represented the only U.N.-sponsored effort to address Internet regulation.) Regional agreements should clearly state that freedom of expression principles apply to electronic communication. These agreements should clarify that the Internet differs significantly from broadcast media in areas such as the level of choice and control afforded to the individual user.

Because of such distinctions, it is important that the Internet not be subject to the same restrictions as are often imposed on broadcast media.

It is important to promote the universal application of two important free expression principles not yet codified in international law. The first of these is an explicit prohibition against prior censorship, that is, requiring official approval of communication before making it public. Such a practice has been used by repressive governments against the press and could be invoked against electronic communication. The second is an explicit prohibition against restrictions of free expression by indirect methods, such as the abuse of controls over equipment or broadcasting frequencies used in the dissemination of information; or by any other means tending to impede the communication and circulation of ideas and opinions. Controls over newsprint have frequently been used to silence critical publications. Governments are already modernizing their techniques to include modem lines and international Internet connections.

In its February 1995 letter to U.S. Vice President Al Gore on the eve of the G7 Ministerial Conference on the Information Society, Human Rights Watch joined with a number of other organizations in proposing the following principles regarding content, access, and privacy.4 (The American Library Association, American Civil Liberties Union, Article 19, Center for Democracy and Technology, Electronic Frontiers Foundation, Electronic Privacy Information Center, People for the American Way, Privacy International also signed the letter.) These principles are even more critical today, and we urge policy makers at the G7 conference in South Africa, and the framers of GII policy within other regional bodies and international organizations, to follow them.

Policy makers should take the initiative to expressly enshrine freedom of expression as a principle in the development of the GII. This should include:

— Prohibiting prior censorship of on-line communication on the GII.

— Demanding that any restrictions of on-line speech content be clearly stated in the law and limited to direct and immediate incitement of acts of violence.

— Requiring that laws restricting the content of on-line speech distinguish between the liability of content providers and the liability of data carriers.

— Insisting that on-line free expression not be restricted by indirect means such as excessively restrictive governmental or private controls over computer hardware or software, telecommunications infrastructure, or other essential components of the GII.

— Calling for the promotion of noncommercial public discourse on the GII.

— Promoting the wide dissemination of diverse ideas and viewpoints from a wide variety of information sources on the GII.

— Ensuring that the GII enable individuals to organize and form on-line associations freely and without interference.

GII policy should emphasize the importance of providing Internet access to everyone, regardless of geographic or other factors. This should encompass:

— Including citizens in the GII development process from countries that are currently unstable economically, have insufficient infrastructure, or lack sophisticated technology.

— Providing nondiscriminatory access to on-line technology.

— Guaranteeing a full range of viewpoints, by providing access to a diversity of information providers, including noncommercial educational, artistic, and other public interest service providers.

— Providing two-way communication and enabling individuals to publish their own information and ideas.

— Protecting diversity of access by establishing technical standards that can be applied easily in a variety of systems.

— Prohibiting discrimination on the basis of race, color, sex, language, religion, political or other opinion, national or social origin, property, birth or other status.

Privacy Issues

Delegates to the G7 meeting and other meetings concerning policy on the GII should guarantee respect for the privacy of communication on the Internet by:

— Ensuring that personal information generated on the GII for one purpose is not used for an unrelated purpose or disclosed without the person's informed consent.

— Enabling individuals to review personal information on the GII and to correct inaccurate information.

— Providing privacy measures for information regarding on-line business transactions as well as content.

— Allowing users of the GII to encrypt their communications and information without restriction.

The above recommendations are also pertinent to individual governments in shaping their own policies with respect to on-line communication. In addition, the following recommendations apply to domestic Internet policies:

— To ensure that domestic Internet services are designed to ensure universal access, governments should provide full disclosure of information infrastructure development plans and encourage democratic participation in all aspects of the development process. They should also advocate widespread use of the GII and strive to provide adequate training. In addition, governments should urge citizens to take an active role in public affairs by providing access to government information.

— In order to guarantee the privacy of on-line communication, governments should put in place enforceable legal protections against unauthorized scrutiny and use by private or public entities of personal information on the GII. They should also oppose controls on the export and import of communications technologies, including encryption. In addition, governments should conduct investigations on the GII pursuant only to lawful authority and subject to judicial review.

The Internet began in the 1960s as a way of linking a U.S. Defense Department network and other communications networks. Over time, many other networks and users from around the world have connected themselves to the Internet. The U.S. still dominates the Internet in terms of users and content, but Canada, Europe, Australia, and New Zealand are also on-line in large numbers. Internet usage in much of Asia is increasing rapidly as well. The number of Internet users is believed to range between twenty and thirty million. More than 160 countries are reported to have links to the Internet, over one hundred nations with full access and the rest through e-mail. (Johanna Son, "Asia-Communication: Bumps Lie Ahead in Information Superhighway," Inter Press Service, December 14, 1995.

The Internet is composed of a number of different ways of organizing, transmitting and accessing data. Because of this multiplicity of systems, it is unlike any other single medium. Rather, it incorporates characteristics of several other media and communications systems, including print, broadcast, and postal systems. Electronic mail (e-mail) allows for one-to-one or one-to-many communication. Gopher sites provide text-only information arranged according to menus. The World Wide Web allows for the display of many types of information, including text, images, sound and video, as well as interactive communication.

A recognition by world leaders of the need to formulate policy for this powerful new medium prompted members of the G7 to hold a "Ministerial Conference on the Information Society" in Brussels in February 1995. At that conference, a number of principles were agreed to, including encouraging competition and private investment, defining an adaptable regulatory framework, providing open access to networks, ensuring universal access, and promoting equality of opportunity and diversity of content. Although freedom of expression was not highlighted in specific terms, to the disappointment of Human Rights Watch and other groups that had urged such an emphasis, it is implied in the final goal promoting diversity of content which can be achieved only by encouraging free expression for people all over the world. (Letter to Vice President Gore from Human Rights Watch, Electronic Privacy Information Center, ACLU, American Library Association, Article 19, Center for Democracy and Technology, Electronic Frontiers Foundation, People for the American Way, and Privacy International, February 16, 1995.) In his keynote address to the conference, Vice President Gore, an active proponent of the GII, stated, "[Global communication] is about protecting and enlarging freedom of expression for all our citizens and giving individual citizens the power to create the information they need and want from the abundant flow of data they encounter moment to moment."

One of the main targets of the censors is Usenet, a system separate from the Internet but accessible from it, that "pump[s] upwards of 100 million characters a day into the system—nearly an encyclopedia's worth of writing." (Adam Gaffin, EFF Guide to the Internet Usenet comprises more than 9,000 "newsgroups" discussions or picture databases on various topics, including the political and the sexually explicit. The groups are arranged under headings such as biz (business), comp (computers and related subjects), rec (hobbies, games and recreation), sci (science), soc ("social" groups, often ethnically related), talk (politics and related topics), and alt (for alternative, often controversial). Not all the newsgroups are available on all.

Internet host computers. Usenet came to prominent international attention most recently in late December 1995, when CompuServe, an on-line service of H&R; Block, based in Columbus, Ohio, removed from all of its computers more than 200 Usenet computer discussion groups and picture databases that had provoked criticism by a federal prosecutor in Munich. (The "banned" newsgroups were still available to CompuServe users who used the service to connect to computers that carried the newsgroups. Information on how to do this circulated quickly through the CompuServe system.) Three days later, the Chinese government echoed the Germans' actions by calling for a crackdown on the Internet to rid the country of pornography and "detrimental information."

It should not be surprising that governments around the globe are anxious to control this new medium. Every communications advance in history has been seen by self-appointed moral guardians as something to be controlled and regulated. By 1558, a century after the invention of the printing press, a Papal index barred the works of more than 500 authors. In 1915, the same year that the D. W. Griffith film "Birth of a Nation" changed the U.S. cultural landscape, the U.S. Supreme Court upheld the constitutionality of an Ohio state censorship board created two years earlier, thus exempting motion pictures from free speech protection on the grounds that their exhibition "is a business, pure and simple, originated and conducted for profit...." The same view was applied in the early days of radio entertainment programs were thought to be exempt from freedom of speech guarantees.

The Internet, as the first truly "mass" medium, is even more threatening than these earlier media. While few individuals and groups can publish books or newspapers, make a film, or produce a radio or television program, any person with a personal computer and a modem can communicate with a huge international audience. The implications of a real GII for the advancement of human rights and democracy are vast. When traditional means of communication broke down and the war in Sarajevo made it impossible for civilians to leave their homes without risking their lives, many citizens used on-line technology to communicate with family members, the international press, and humanitarian relief agencies. Human rights groups, political organizations, and builders of burgeoning democracies are using the Internet to communicate, educate, and organize. During the United Nations Fourth World Conference on Women, held in Beijing in 1995, women all over the world were able to feel a sense of participation because of regular postings on the proceedings. It is precisely because of the Internet's potential for increasing the political participation of the disenfranchised that governments are seeking to control it.

These initial achievements could easily disappear if the censors are allowed to have their way. Governments and other institutions that support freedom of expression must ensure that the Internet is granted the same guarantees that are given to other forms of individual expression. International law is clear on what electronic rights of expression must entail. Although international law does not address such communication specifically, the Universal Declaration on Human Rights and the International Covenant on Civil and Political Rights enshrine rights to freedom of expression, access, and privacy, which are relevant to the new medium. Article 19 of the Universal Declaration of Human Rights proclaims:

Everyone has the right to freedom of opinion and expression; this right includes freedom to hold opinions without interference and to seek, receive and impart information and ideas through any media and regardless of frontiers. (Other relevant articles from the Universal Declaration of Human Rights include the following: "Article 7: All are equal before the law and are entitled without any discrimination to equal protection of the law; Article 12: No one shall be subjected to arbitrary interference with his privacy, family, home or correspondence; Article 27: Everyone has the right freely to participate in the cultural life of the community, to enjoy the arts and to share in scientific advancement and its benefits.)

Article 19 of the International Covenant on Civil and Political Rights (ICCPR) guarantees this right as well, and notes that restrictions on this right "shall only be such as are provided by law and are necessary:

— "For respect of the rights or reputations of others;

— "For the protection of national security or of public order (ordre public), or of public health or morals."(Other relevant articles from the ICCPR include the following: Article 25 guarantees the right "to take part in the conduct of public affairs;" Article 26 states: "All persons are equal before the law and are entitled without any discrimination to equal protection of the law....[T]he law shall prohibit any discrimination and guarantee to all persons equal and effective protection against discrimination on any ground such as race, color, sex, language, religion, political or other opinion, national or social origin, property, birth or other status.")

The recently adopted Johannesburg Principles on National Security, Freedom of Expression and Access to Information (These Principles were adopted on October 1, 1995 by a group of experts in international law, national security, and human rights.) state that restrictions on freedom of expression are permitted only when "the government can demonstrate that the restriction is prescribed by law and is necessary in a democratic society to protect a legitimate national security interest." (For the purposes of the Principles, "a democratic society is one which has a government that is genuinely accountable to an entity or organ distinct from itself; there must be genuine, periodic elections by universal and equal suffrage held by secret ballot that guarantee the free expression of the will of the electors; political groups must be free to organize in opposition to the government in office; and there must be effective legal guarantees of fundamental rights enforced by an independent judiciary.") According to the Principles, the burden of demonstrating the validity of the restriction rests with the government. (Principle 1(c).) Criticism of the government or its leaders is protected. (Principle 7.) In addition, a government must demonstrate that "the restriction imposed is the least restrictive means possible for protecting that interest."

North America

Hysteria about "cyberporn" was ignited in the U.S. after Time magazine published a cover story, complete with lurid photographs, asserting the wide availability of sexually explicit material on the Internet. (Philip Elmer-Dewitt, "On a Screen Near You: It's Popular, Pervasive and Surprisingly Perverse, According to the First Survey of On-line Erotica. And There's No Easy Way To Stamp It Out," Time, July 3, 1995.) The article was based on the research findings (later acknowledged by Time to have been seriously flawed) of a student at Carnegie Mellon University. Nevertheless, this concern recently culminated in the enactment of the Communications Decency Act (CDA), an amendment to a sweeping telecommunications reform bill signed in February 1996.

The CDA criminalizes on-line communication that is "obscene, lewd, lascivious, filthy, or indecent, with intent to annoy, abuse, threaten, or harass an other person" or "obscene or indecent" if the recipient of the communication is under eighteen years of age "regardless of whether the maker of such communication placed the call or initiated the communication."

Also prohibited is on-line communication to minors that "depicts or describes, in terms patently offensive as measured by contemporary community standards, sexual or excretory activities or organs, regardless of whether the user of such service placed the call or initiated the communication." The CDA would permit the U.S., for example, to seek the arrest of a European content provider whose sexually explicit material was seen as "indecent" or "patently offensive."

In letters to members of Congress and President Clinton, Human Rights Watch opposed the CDA, taking the position that "indecent" speech is protected by both the U.S. Constitution and international law. Human Rights Watch is also concerned that the effort to censor "indecent" communication could impede the work of our own and similar organizations which transmit graphic accounts of human rights abuses. Because of these concerns, in February, Human Rights Watch became a plaintiff in a lawsuit brought by the American Civil Liberties Union challenging the CDA on constitutional grounds. The suit is currently before a panel of judges. According to our affidavit,

Some of the accounts are necessarily graphic and explicit: torture, rape, mutilation, execution, mass murder are brutalities that must be discussed in detail if people are to understand the widespread human rights abuses occurring worldwide. Likewise, to address human rights abuses without discussing the violence of acts such as rape, torture, and bodily mutilation would be impossible. Human Rights Watch exposes the abuse in order to educate the public about the scope of current abuse and to prevent future atrocities.

The graphic nature of some of the eyewitness accounts, especially those dealing with sexual assault, may be considered "indecent" or "patently offensive" under this statute. For example, our July 1995 press release on slavery in Pakistan, posted at our gopher site [on the Internet], provides graphic and factual details on the ways in which bonded laborers have been tortured. The text relates that they have been "beaten with sticks, stripped naked, hung upside down, burned with cigarettes, beaten on the genitals and have had their legs pulled apart. Women prisoners are often held in custody indefinitely and suffer a consistent pattern of sexual assault, including rape."

A March 1995 press release on abuses by Nigerian security forces in Ogoniland, posted at our gopher site, quotes the testimony of one woman, as follows: "K, a woman in her late thirties from the village of Bera, told Human Rights Watch that she had been raped by five soldiers in rapid succession on the morning of May 28,

1994. After locking K's 10-year-old son in a room, K recalled, the soldiers beat me with the butts of their guns, pushed me onto the ground, and kicked me. They tore off my wrapper, then my underwear. Two of them raped me through my anus, three the usual way. While one soldier raped me, another would beat me. I tried to scream, but they held my mouth. They said if I made too much noise they would kill me.

Our October 1993 report on the abuse of Burmese refugees from Arakan, posted on the newsgroup reg.seasia, relates abuses against women in language such as, "then the official grabbed her breast"; "the CIC and the other official put their hands inside S.K.'s clothing and touched her all over her body, including her vagina"; "...one policeman fondled S.K.'s breasts and struck S.K. on the back of then neck with a stick".

Clearly, obstacles to Human Rights Watch in reporting these atrocities in the United States are likely to be magnified for groups operating in more repressive states and attempting to post similar findings on the Internet.

Canada

In response to the debate about cyberspace, the Canadian government formed the Information Highway Advisory Council (IHAC) in 1994 to study and prepare an official statement on what directions the Internet should take in Canada. In September 1995, the council released its first report, which contained only vague recommendations. On the issue of content, it concluded that there should be controls on two primary targets: obscenity and racist/ hate material. It is illegal to spread "hate propaganda" and "obscenity" in Canada. Sexually explicit material is legal as long as it is not deemed obscene, that is, characterized by "undue exploitation of sex," meaning sex plus violence or degrading sex. Under a new law on child pornography that has not been tested by the Supreme Court, mere possession is illegal. According to David Jones, president of

Electronic Frontiers Canada, "There are no new laws being proposed that apply specifically to the Internet." That could change, however. On April 2, 1996, Justice Minister Allan Rock released a discussion paper inviting Canadians to present their views on regulating excessive violence in the media, including the Internet.

Asia

Asia now has over 1.5 million users, two-thirds of them in Japan. (Johanna Son, "Asia-Communication: Bumps Lie Ahead in Information Superhighway," Inter Press Service, December 14, 1995.) Among the region's authoritarian nations, only North Korea and Myanmar are without any Internet connection. (Philip Shenon, "Why Nations Fear the Net," New York Times, June 11, 1995.) Currently, most countries in Asia are connected directly to the U.S., rather than to each other, but new initiatives have proposed establishing an intra-Asia connection.

Some Asian governments, including Pakistan, are choosing to control the Internet's effects mainly by limiting its availability. A senior scientist at Pakistan's state-owned National Institute of Electronics has noted that Internet access would be limited by the small number of nodes and hosts available to users and by the intervention of service providers who could stop undesirable discussion groups and electronic messages.24

In India, where commercial Internet access was launched in mid-1995, only the state-owned phone company, VSNL, has been allowed to provide international Internet services, in order to maintain the government's monopoly on long-distance phone services.

According to guidelines issued by the Department of Telecommunications (DoT) based on the antiquated Indian Telegraph Act of 1885, an ISP must ensure that nothing objectionable or obscene is carried on the network, but it is not clear that these have been enforced. In late January 1996, the DoT decided to allow commercial access, but all companies will have to route their services through VSNL.

Thailand's National Electronics and Computer Technology Center (Nectec), an official agency responsible for information technology policy, recently called upon local ISPs to police their own sites for sexually explicit material. It also said that subscribers and operators are required to agree not to show anything considered indecent or they will face criminal prosecution. (Nigel Armstrong and I.T. Daily, "Thai Group on Porn Trail," Newsbytes News Network, February 26, 1996.) In the Philippines, Internet censorship measures have been introduced in the legislature.28 (Ninez Cacho-Olivares, "My Cup of Tea Pornography on the Net," Business World (Manilla), March 18, 1996.)

In early March 1996, member nations of the Association of Southeast Asian Nations (ASEAN) said they planned to set up a regulatory body to deal with the flood of information technology; they also voiced concern about pornography and disinformation. (Ramthan

Hussein, "Singapore Deputy Premier Defends\ Curbs on Internet," Reuters, March 9, 1996.)

China

Commercial Internet accounts became available in China in mid-1995, but at prices far beyond the means of all but the wealthiest. In June 1995, China's telecommunications minister stated that "as a sovereign state, China will exercise control on the information" entering China from the Internet. "By linking with the Internet, we do not mean the absolute freedom of information." Many Usenet newsgroups, including those classified as alt, rec and soc, were reportedly not allowed on Chinese Internet host computers, but the comp and sci hierarchies were apparently provided.

The Hong Kong-based China Internet Corporation (CIC), principally owned by China's state-run Xinhua News Agency, offers Chinese business subscribers only limited access to business-related information. Users have access to information generated outside China, but only after it has been screened in Hong Kong. According to James Chu, CEO of CIC, customers can be assured their e-mail will not be screened or bugged by mainland "unless you have broken the law."

ChinaNet, based in Beijing and Shanghai, which became available in May 1995, provided commercial Internet access. Control of Internet access accounts was extremely tight, and people wishing to open them were required to register at the Postal Ministry. Fairly quickly, black market permits became available.

On January 1, 1996, several days after CompuServe cut off access to 200 Usenet newsgroups, Xinhua News Agency, China's official medium, reported that the government had called for a crackdown on the Internet to rid the country of unwanted pornography and "detrimental information." A joint statement issued by the State Council and the Communist Party Central Committee said effective measures had to be adopted to solve the problem of uncontrolled information. The leadership also reportedly summoned the Chinese suppliers of Internet connections, and on January 15, the biggest supplier announced a "moratorium" on new subscribers.

According to press reports, officials said that as many as 70,000 people were using the Internet through 7,000 accounts, and that the high volume was more than the current system could handle. On January 23, a cabinet session chaired by Premier Li Peng adopted draft rules governing links to the Internet. The cabinet reiterated its provisional approval for global computer links but declared it "imperative" to formulate rules to govern China's use of the new technology. On February 4, Xinhua announced that the new Internet regulations required existing computer networks to "liquidate" and "re-register," and to use only international channels provided by the Ministry of Posts and Telecommunications, the Ministry of Electronics Industry, the State Education Commission and the Chinese Academy of Sciences.

Neither organizations nor individuals are allowed to engage in activities at the expense of state security and secrets," [Xinhua] said. "They are also forbidden to produce, retrieve, duplicate or spread information that may hinder public order. The transmission of pornographic or obscene material was also expressly banned. In mid-February, the Ministry of Public Security ordered all those who use the Internet and other international computer networks to register with the police within thirty days.

Hong Kong

Hong Kong has not drafted any policy or released any official statements regarding Internet censorship. The 1987 Obscene and Indecent Articles Ordinance does not specifically discuss on-line communication, but the ordinance reportedly applies to communication on the Internet. The Hong Kong government's Recreation and Culture Branch, which oversees on-line media, recently commissioned a study of on-line communication. Its secretary said that developments in other countries, including the United States, would be taken into account.

There are currently more than fifty Hong Kong ISPs, and some censor content, including Hong Kong SuperNet, one of the largest Hong Kong ISPs, which voluntarily ended access to sexually explicit material on Usenet in March 1995. Star Internet followed suit in November, by blocking about twenty newsgroups with erotic text and pictures.

In March 1996, Commissioner of the Television and Entertainment Licensing Authority Peter Cheung Po-tak said that controls on the Internet should ensure a "minimum degree of decency" to protect children and said the best solution would be for ISPs to regulate themselves.

Singapore

In Singapore the Internet is treated as a broadcast medium, regulated under the Singapore Broadcasting Authority Act of 1995, which established the Singapore Broadcasting Authority (SBA). Singapore allows three service providers: Singnet, which is part of Singapore Telecom, Pacific Internet and Cyberway. The government claims that it does not currently censor e-mail, but in 1994 it disclosed that it had searched individual accounts to try to identify those who had downloaded sexually explicit material. After businesses expressed alarmed about the security of their information, authorities said they would refrain from conducting such searches in the future.

The main means of censorship up to now has been to control access. In addition, sexually explicit material and news have been censored by the Ministry of Information and the Arts, the government body in charge of media censorship. Fewer than half of Usenet newsgroups are available through Singnet. Currently there are no widespread uniform guidelines or procedures for restricting use of any Internet services, and local administrators have to make arbitrary decision on access.

The minister of information and the arts told Parliament that "Censorship can no longer be 100 percent effective, but even if it is only 20 percent effective, we should still not stop censoring....We cannot screen every bit of information that comes down the information highway, but we can make it illegal and costly for mass distributors of objectionable material to operate in Singapore." Colonel Ho Meng Kit, the CEO of the SBA, the committee that oversees content on the Internet, said objectionable material could be censored through three main channels: technology, legislation, and licensing. He stated that only ISPs would be targeted and noted, "[Censorship] may not always be effective but it makes a statement about the nature of Singapore society and the values it wants to uphold."

Although authorities initially stated that they would not heavily censor political criticism, they have reportedly shifted from watching for sex-related material to watching for "misinformation." Some topics recently discussed on the newsgroup soc.culture.singapore ranging from Michael Fay's caning to the case of a Filipino maid convicted of double murder sparked the formation of a government administrative committee, which has started

Singapore Infomap, a Web site, to provide "correct" information and rebut "inaccurate" information.

In early March, the government announced more severe censorship measures, including the licensing of all ISPs and a requirement to use filtering software. The measures are meant to prevent Singaporeans from accessing sexually explicit material and hate literature, and will also cover politics and religion. The government also announced that World Wide Web content providers would have to register with the SBA, and that three categories of Web pages would be scrutinized: those operated by political parties, electronic newspapers targeting Singapore, and pages concerned with politics or religion. In April, the regulations tightened further. The SBA announced that it was setting guidelines, to become effective in June 1996, for Internet content providers.

According to the preliminary guidelines, those with Web sites must ensure they do not encourage abuse or distribute objectionable information, such as sexually explicit material. Sponsors of discussion groups may have to register with the SBA. Internet content providers and ISPs will be responsible for what is transmitted. The rules also require Internet service providers to institute an acceptable use policy.

Indonesia

Indonesia's first commercial provider, Indonet, began operation in late 1994. A number of others soon followed, and the country now has numerous ISPs. The more established electronic bulletin board networks also draw extensively from the Internet. The Internet is more free than any other mass medium in Indonesia, and there are no laws, regulations or ministerial decrees concerning its use. Tempo, a news weekly that was closed by the government two years ago, recently established a site on the Web, with the blessing of the minister of information who agreed "there are no regulations against it," but warned that "maybe the House [of Representatives] will want to discuss legislating the Internet." At this stage, however, the government has chosen to compete with opposing views by establishing its own Web sites.

Armed Forces spokesman Brig.-Gen. Surwarno Adiwijoyo told Reuters news agency that the military had suggested to the Communications Ministry the need for some sort of "toll gate" to "black out" news that could damage culture or affect security. It has also suggested registering uses and users, he said. At present, private ISPs do not carry all Usenet groups, but this is reportedly done in the interests of conserving disk space and because of the language barrier.

Malaysia

The Malaysian Institute of Microelectronic Systems (Mimos), the nation's sole Internet provider, has experienced a huge demand, with an average monthly increase of 22 percent since it began service in late 1994. As of October 1995, there were some 30,000 users. In April 1996, Mimos announced that it would appoint eight new ISPs to help ease congestion.

Usenet newsgroups are heavily censored. The "acceptable use" policy at Jaring, the main Malaysian Internet line, states that "members shall not use Jaring network for any activities not allowed under any Law of Malaysia." (Charles A. Gimon, "Internet Censorship Around the World," Info Nation (Minneapolis, MN), July 1995.) The government reportedly realizes that on-line censorship may not be effective. Prime Minister Datuk Seri Dr. Mahathir Mohamad has warned Malaysians that "It depends on the culture. If the culture is weak, we will be the victims. But if we use it in a way that can increase our knowledge, we will get many benefits from the Internet."However, in March 1996, Information Minister Datuk Mohamed Rahmat announced that a new regulatory body would be set up to monitor the Internet and that those criticizing the government "will face the music."

In reaction to Malaysian students abroad criticizing Malaysia on the Internet, the government has considered various ways to curb such dissent, according to the information and education ministers, and the education minister proposed cutting scholarships of offending students.

South Korea

In South Korea, about half of all Internet users are affiliated with universities or the government. The nationally run telephone corporation, Korea Telecom, started service in June 1994, and there are a number of other commercial providers.

The government has decided to censor computer networks, according to statements by communications officials in October 1995. The decision was reportedly made out of growing concern regarding children's access to sexually explicit and other undesirable material. Local computer networks will be asked to prohibit access by local subscribers to banned sites, according to the Information and Communications Ethics Committee of the Data and Communications Ministry. Sexually explicit material will be banned, along with information deemed "subversive," such as instructions on making bombs and drugs. Computer games and other software are already censored. Details, such as punishments, have reportedly yet to be worked out.

Vietnam

The state-owned telecommunications company Vietnam Datacommunications Company (VDC) had planned to launch Internet service earlier this year, but it reportedly put off the opening day because officials decided to first draft regulations on allowable Internet links and users. Internet regulations will reportedly comply with the government's existing censorship regulations. Pham Dao, director of VDC, said that an Internet firewall would be installed to screen out transmissions from specified senders or news resources cutting out much of the anti-government commentary carried by dissident groups, including support for jailed Buddhists and dissidents.56 It appears likely that the Ministry of Culture and Information will monitor on-line content and that Interior Ministry will be in charge of monitoring Internet national security issues. Nguyen Ngoc Canh of the General Directorate of Posts and Telecommunications, which sets communication policy, said competing domestic services likely will be allowed as long as Vietnam Datacommunications Company monitors a single outside link.

Until recently, Vietnam's Internet service was made available through the Institute of Information Technology, which exists mostly for the benefit of academics and nongovernmental organizations. A VDC official told the press that the organization's effort to control the Internet "is the requirement from our leaders, our government. The Internet must be controlled, not only for technical and security reasons but from the cultural aspect." The government is reportedly worried about sexually explicit material from foreign countries and about "foreign organizations" transmitting information. Some overseas Vietnamese groups have distributed anti-government tracts in Hanoi. Prime Minister Vo Van Kiet was recently the victim of "spamming" (an e-mail barrage) by anti-communist dissidents in the U.S.

Australia and New Zealand

Australia has been considering regulating the Internet since 1993. In August 1994, the Department of Communications and the Arts released a report, "Regulation of Computer Bulletin Board Systems," which called for regulations. A year later, the recommendations in that report were updated and released in the "Consultation Paper on the Regulation of On-line Information Services." One of the goals elucidated in the consultation paper was "to protect freedom of expression, especially with regard to private communication between adults, while at the same time limiting children's exposure to harmful or unsuitable material." It proposed a system of self-regulation reinforced by legislative sanctions.

Objectionable material was defined in the consultation paper as material that "depicts, expresses, or otherwise deals with matters of sex, drug misuse or addiction, crime, cruelty, violence or revolting or abhorrent phenomena in such a way that it offends against the standards of morality, decency and proprietary generally accepted by reasonable adults to the extent that the material should be refused classification." Restricted material was defined as "material that [is] unsuitable for seeing, reading or playing by persons under 15."

In August 1995, the minister for communications and the arts directed the Australian Broadcasting Authority (ABA), an independent federal authority responsible for the regulation of the broadcasting industry, to investigate the content of on-line information and entertainment services and report to him by June 30,

1996. The resulting ABA "issues paper" became available in December 1995, with an invitation for comments to be submitted by the public until mid-February. The paper discusses various issues involved in the development of a code of practice, the adoption of a classification scheme, enforcement of a code, and blocking offensive sites.

Electronic Frontiers Australia, a nongovernmental organization working for rights of Internet users in Australia, submitted a response to the issues paper, arguing a number of points, including that the Internet, because of its interactivity, significantly differs from broadcast media. "Classification of content is unnecessary and in most instances impossible to police," it pointed out. The EFA also urged the government to consult with the industry and "develop a grasp of the realities of the on-line service industry."

Some state governments, including those of New South Wales, Queensland, Victoria, Western Australia, Northern Territory, and Tasmania, have already passed or are planning to introduce on-line censorship legislation. In early October 1995, eighteen people were being questioned and fifteen computers seized across the state of Queensland for alleged involvement with child pornography, based on the state's Classification of Computer Games and Images Act. In Victoria state, the Classification. Bill, which has passed two houses of Parliament and awaits enactment, makes it an offense to use an on-line network to transmit "objectionable" material to minors. Victoria's bill has passed two houses of Parliament. A similar law in Western Australia went into effect on January 1, 1996. Both leave primary censorship in the hands of service providers, and seek to punish senders of information deemed "objectionable" and senders of information classified as "restricted" to minors according to broad definitions contained in the legislation. ISPs are liable only if they knowingly permit objectionable material to be transmitted on their network. An even more extreme bill now before the parliament in New South Wales will hold individuals and ISPs responsible for objectionable material, which includes not only sexually explicit information but also drug- and crime-related material. All state laws are subject to change when new federal laws are adopted.

New Zealand

Restrictive Internet legislation was proposed in Parliament in 1994, but, according to Stephen Bell, an Internet activist in New Zealand, it "is widely perceived as more or less dead" at present because of unrelated political developments. Under the legislation, the New Zealand Technology and Crimes Reform Bill, all users would be cut off from any site that transmitted a single piece of objectionable material to a single user. Those found in violation of the law could be fined thousands and lose the use of a telephone for up to five years.

Under current law, computer disks are treated as "publications," and may be censored as such under the Films, Videos and Publications Classification Act of 1993. If authorities find one example of the more serious grade of "objectionable" material, as defined by the Act,67 ("Objectionable" is defined to include that which "describes, depicts, expresses, or otherwise deals with matters such as sex, horror, crime, cruelty, or violence in such a manner that the availability of the publication is likely to be injurious to the public good.") they may arrest and shut down an ISP.

Apparently fearing possible liability, several universities and Internet providers have been blocking access to newsgroups dealing with erotica.

Middle East

The Middle East is coming on-line in increasing numbers, but many governments are hoping to control access to sensitive political and religious discussion as well as sex-related material. Bahrain went on-line in December 1995 through Batelco, the government-run phone company, after installing an expensive system to block access to certain Internet-related sites. GlobeNet, a U.S. firm, won a contract to provide Internet service in Jordan in 1995 and was asked by authorities to install a special screening facility to control sexually explicit material. Kuwait is planning to launch a new Internet service soon, but a Communications Ministry official told the press that the new ISP "must ensure that no pornography or politically subversive' commentary is available in Kuwait." There is no new content-related legislation planned at present. In Abu Dhabi, an Internet club "ha[s] agreed to ban sex, religion and politics on the Internet to respect the local laws." Police in the United Arab Emirates recently held a seminar on combatting political dissent and sexually explicit material.

In Morocco, the state Office National des Postes et Telecommunications (ONPT) brought the Internet to the nation on November 16, 1995. ONPT has secured an agreement with the commercial companies that will provide the service. Charges will be fixed, and a convention has been signed to govern all aspects of the Internet's operation. The service has been targeted at the banking and insurance sectors, universities, and multinational corporations.

Iran

The first Iranian Internet line was opened in 1992 by the Institute for Studies in Theoretical Physics and Mathematics through a link to Vienna. The government helped with funds. Internet users, still mostly at universities, now number around 30,000.

The government also sponsors a network whose chat rooms allow on-line dialogue between only two subscribers at a time, and private ISPs also exist. Access to the Internet is relatively unregulated, but its increasing popularity will likely result in greater government control. One private network had its lines cut by the Telecommunications Company (TCI) of Iran in August 1995. TCI may have been reacting to reports that the network was being used by young people for sex chats, or it may have been trying to reduce competition to its own network service.

Saudi Arabia

In Saudi Arabia, Internet access has been confined to universities and hospitals. All local accounts, which automatically note the material accessed, are open to inspection by the Ministry of the Interior. Government officials have justified their reluctance to permit large-scale access on the grounds that there is a need to protect people from pornographic and other harmful effects. Existing pornography laws apply to the Internet, but loopholes are available: large foreign companies are increasingly offering their unmonitored Internet access to Saudi business acquaintances, and commercial members of the GulfNet are also free from scrutiny.

Internet access will reportedly be made available to businesses in 1996, but reportedly with strict controls. Mohammed Benten, a dean at King Fahd University for Petroleum and Minerals in Dhahran, told a local newspaper, "Here in the kingdom, with our strict rules and regulations, we will see the Internet being accessed only for constructive objectives." Minister of Posts, Telephones and Telegraphs Dr. Ali Al-Johani said in February 1996 that, although the Internet was beyond government control, authorities were investigating how it could be regulated.

Europe

The European Union is considering adopting some Internet-related controls. In late January 1996, a European Union Consultative Commission on Racism and Xenophobia said it "hope[d] the EU [would] take all needed measures to prevent Internet from becoming a vehicle for the incitement of racist hatred." It also called for the "creation of protective judicial measures." It urged all member states to follow the example of Germany, which has been trying to censor racist and pornographic messages. France joined the call for regulation in early February, when the French minister for information technology announced that France would request members of the EU to draft new legislation to cope with legal issues posed by the Internet. It is believed that France's reaction has to do with the recent posting on the Internet of the banned book, Le Grand Secret, by Claude Gubler, the late President Mitterand's physician.

EU culture and telecommunications ministers met informally in Bologna, Italy in late April 1996, to discuss Internet regulation. At the meeting, France proposed the drafting of a global convention on Internet regulation. The ministers agreed to ask the European Commission, the executive body of the EU, to draw up a report on the question. The Commission is reportedly supposed to determine whether the EU should deal with this issue, or whether the issue should proceed directly to international negotiations.

That same week in Strasbourg, Irish Minister of State for European Affairs Gay Mitchell called on the EU to investigate controls on the transmission of child pornography on the Internet at a joint meeting organized by UNICEF and the Council of Europe, to discuss the commercial exploitation of children.

The European Commission reportedly plans to draft a discussion paper on interactive services, including the Internet, which may lead to a directive that may include content regulation. The European Commission is considering a regulation requiring EU member states to send draft national legislation affecting the Internet to the EU in order for member states to vet the laws before they are adopted. The European Commission is reportedly divided over how to standardize Internet policies of its member states. The European Parliament has introduced changes to the EU's broadcasting law to extend its scope to the Internet, but that approach is strongly opposed by many in the computer industry.

United Kingdom The UK has not yet enacted any Internet-specific censorship legislation but has relied, instead, on existing laws banning obscenity. Gay groups, however, reportedly feel they are being victimized. An organizer for the London-based group, S&M; Gays, for example, told the press that "The police seem to have great difficulty in distinguishing between gay men and pedophiles."

The group closed down its computer bulletin board, fearing that it might become a police target. In its recent proposals for media ownership, the UK government suggested that the media industry regulator could have some influence over the content of the Internet. An inter-departmental group was set up in March 1995 to examine tackling such issues as sexually explicit material on the Internet. A new defamation bill extending libel to computer networks was introduced in February 1996; it provides a defense for ISPs as long as they are do not knowingly permit a defamatory statement to be made over their networks. On-line service providers have asked the government for further clarification on their responsibilities under the legislation.

In March 1996, British Trade and Industry Minister Ian Taylor said the UK was seeking a voluntary approach to regulation of content on the Internet. The Internet Service Providers Association (ISPA), a voluntary grouping of service providers to be formally launched in May 1996, is drawing up a code of practice that will cover fair trading issues, and Taylor said that he expected the code to cover "both illegal and undesirable material." He added, "The only alternative to voluntary action ... is increased political pressure for legislation in various areas. That pressure may get increasingly hard to resist."

France

On March 15, 1996, French ISPs were subpoenaed after a

French Jewish student organization brought charges against them for alleged "complicity" in making available propaganda that denies the Holocaust; such propaganda is illegal in France. A decision was to be reached in April, as this report went to press.

Germany

Germany and CompuServe have both been criticized for their roles in the CompuServe censorship episode. CompuServe and the German officials involved have made conflicting statements regarding who actually made the decision to censor Usenet newsgroups. As far as Human Rights Watch has been able to determine, a task force was set up by the Bavarian minister of the interior at police headquarters in Munich in 1994 to search for on-line child pornography.

The task force obtained a search warrant to investigate the Munich CompuServe office on November 22, 1995. The search was reportedly more like a visit, in which the authorities told the company of their concerns and CompuServe agreed to comply. Two days later, CompuServe's German managers reportedly stated that they would support German authorities' fight against pornography in cyberspace. On December 8, the authorities gave them a list of more than 200 suggested newsgroups with a letter saying "...it is left to CompuServe to take the necessary steps to avoid possible liabilities to punishment." CompuServe then made the decision to take all the groups off its servers, apparently without making the effort to look at them. Among the groups it "banned" were discussion groups for homosexuals and the news service Clarinet, which was not even on its servers.

As with other instances of Internet censorship, the ban was an ineffective effort to comply with the demands of an ill-informed authority. CompuServe users still of course had access to the Internet and could therefore connect to other host computers that carried the forbidden newsgroups. In February, CompuServe again provided access to the 200 formerly censored newsgroups, except for five groups. The Bavarian minister of justice recently claimed that CompuServe's new Cyber Patrol software does not meet the company's obligations under German law because the company has an obligation not to supply illegal material to German citizens.

Moving from sexually explicit material to hate speech, in January 1996, Deutsche Telekom (DT), the national telephone company, blocked users of its T-Online computer network from accessing Internet sites used to spread anti-Semitic propaganda, which is a crime in Germany. Authorities also announced that they were expanding their investigation to America Online and Deutsche Forschungsnetz, the national scientific research network. The company was responding to demands by Mannheim prosecutors who were investigating Ernst Zuendel, a German-born neo-Nazi living in Toronto.

DT also blocked access to a Santa Cruz, California computer service, Web Communications, that also provides access to Zuendel's site. Web Communications stated that although it did not agree with Zuendel, it was not the company's policy to censor its users. A DT spokesman said that access to certain providers was blocked while government prosecutors investigated on-line neo-Nazi material. The lack of organized monitoring by DT is reflected in the fact that Zuendel's Web site was still available through CompuServe at the same time as it was "banned" through Web Communications.

Rita Suessmuth, president of the Bundestag, the German parliament, was recently quoted in German newspapers as saying, "The information superhighway must not be allowed to become a forum for those who defile children." She added, "Freedom of expression reaches its limit when human dignity is violated and violence is promoted."The government reportedly disagrees with her assessment, however. Justice Minister Edzard Schmidt-Jortzig said in late March 1996 that the government would introduce Internet censorship legislation before the summer recess. The legislation will seek to punish an ISP only if it knowingly permits illegal material on its service, but will not expect ISPs to be responsible for all the content on their servers. The legislation is expected to face opposition from the regional states, who plan to contest the measure on constitutional grounds and may propose a more restrictive law.

Latin Amercia

Internet censorship has not become a major issue in Latin America. Latin America is fully connected, except for Paraguay, Haiti, Belize and Cuba. In May 1996, Cuba, which at present has only e-mail service, will hold its first national telecommunications and informatics conference, Ariadna 96, to discuss the Internet. Jesus Martinez, director of the Center for Automated Information Exchange, the server for Cuba's largest e-mail network, says that regulations affecting electronic information connections and security are being studied "that do not anticipate including individuals." He also told the press that Cuba was "studying regulations about connections and security." Rosa Elena Simeon, the minister of science, technology and environment, said in January that Cuba must learn how to "use the Internet's capabilities and advantages while reducing its risks and disadvantages as much as possible." Guyanese officials also reportedly announced that the government "would move to prevent any unauthorized installation' of Internet services and added that they were studying ways of regulating links."

Africa

South Africa's Deputy President Thabo Mbeki pointed out to the G7 conference of wealthy countries that there were more telephone lines in Manhattan, New York than in the whole of sub-Saharan Africa."

In Africa, access, technology and training are the huge hurdles to cross before censorship will be a major issue. As of late 1995, fewer than ten countries were directly connected to the Internet. In those countries, however, government control and censorship have already asserted themselves. As in Asia and the Middle East, some countries, such as Botswana, that have Internet access do not allow private ISPs to operate. The reason is reportedly not so much one of content control, but of money. The government is anxious not to lose the revenue from its monopoly on telecommunications services.

In the southern African country of Zambia, where Internet access is limited, the February 5 Internet edition of The Post, a daily and one of Zambia's most important opposition voices, was banned by President Chiluba under the State Security Act. The charges relate to a report based on leaked documents, revealing secret government plans to hold a referendum on the adoption of a new constitution. It remained on the Web site for two days until the police warned the ISP, Zamnet Communications, that it would be liable.

Rather than striving to control content on the Internet, democratic governments should be working to ensure that the GII becomes truly global, and to motivate citizens to become more involved in decision making as they organize, debate, and share information unrestricted by geographic distances or national borders. It has already been shown that the GII has the potential to:

— permit individuals with common interests to organize themselves in forums to debate public policy issues;

— provide instant access to a wide range of information;

— increase citizen oversight of government affairs;

— decentralize political decision making;

— empower users to become active producers of information rather than passive consumers.

As noted above, although the extraordinary potential for a GII has been suggested by existing on-line communications networks, the present on-line community is still quite limited. Only countries with a sophisticated telecommunications infrastructure are able to take full advantage of on-line technology. Even in countries with advanced telecommunications infrastructures, only persons with access to equipment and training can take advantage of new information resources. General illiteracy remains the primary obstacle to computer literacy. And while the GII may foster an unprecedented sharing of cultural traditions, current users of on-line technology are primarily American or northern European, affluent, white, and male. To maximize the GII's potential to promote democracy, it must adopt and expand upon international standards of free expression. National and international guarantees of free expression should be expressly extended to the Internet.

10

Critical Infrastructure Protection

On July 15, 1997, President Clinton signed Executive Order 13010, which established the President's Commission on Critical Infrastructure Protection (PPCIP). The Executive Order listed eight sectors that the PCCIP was to examine for security vulnerabilities. They are: telecommunications, electrical power systems, gas and oil storage and transportation, banking and finance, transportation, water supply systems, emergency services, and continuity of government.

President Clinton appointed retired Air Force General Robert T. Marsh to chair the PCCIP. Although the commission, its Steering Committee, and its Advisory Committee were composed of members of government and industry, the membership of the three bodies consisted of a majority of military and intelligence representatives. Appendix B lists the military and intelligence affiliated members.

PCCIP's, issued in October 1997, contained many recommendations that have the potential to curtail a number of important civil liberties, including freedom of speech and freedom of information. Although the report concluded there was no evidence of an "impending cyber attack which could have a debilitating effect on the nation's critical infrastructure," it did recommend a new bureaucratic security establishment with expansive authority. If not properly monitored and controlled, these new national security structures and intelligence-sharing networks, in addition to those that already exist, may, instead of protecting the national infrastructure, be used by the government and private corporations to further erode the privacy of U.S. and foreign citizens.

Duane Andrews, a former top Pentagon official who is an executive Vice President at Science Applications International Corporation (SAIC), a large intelligence and military contractor, sees no practical difference. He stated, "A large international bank has exactly the same problems and challenges as the Defense Department."

In response to the PCCIP's report, on May 22, 1998, President Clinton signed two Presidential Decision Directives - PDD 62 (*Combating Terrorism*) and PDD 63 (*Critical Infrastructure Protection*) - designed to defend the nation's critical infrastructures from various threats, including "cyber attacks" by computer hackers and terrorists. The White House summary of these two PDDs is contained in Appendix A. PDD 63 carried out most of the recommendations contained in the Report of the President's Commission. These include the establishment of several new boards and agencies, some with Internet surveillance authority. One of the new offices is the National Coordinator for Security, Infrastructure Protection, and Counter-terrorism within the National Security Council. This office is headed by Richard Clarke, a person who has spent a number of years in intelligence-related functions. Clarke reports to the

President through the Assistant to the President for National Security Affairs.

PDD-63 also authorized the creation of a National Infrastructure Assurance Council (consisting of private sector and state and local government representatives), a National Plan Coordination (NPC) staff, the Critical Infrastructure Assurance Office (CIAO) (headed by Jeffrey Hunker), the Critical Infrastructure Coordination Group (CICG), and the National Infrastructure Protection Center (NIPC) under the FBI. Of most alarm is the fact that the NIPC may be assisted in its Internet surveillance activities by the Department of Defense and the U.S. Intelligence Community. The NIPC is headed by Associate Deputy Attorney General Michael Vatis.

In addition, PDD-63 encourages private industry to establish an Information Sharing and Analysis Center (ISAC). However, the Federal government is authorized to facilitate the start-up of the ISAC. Many observers believe that the NSA's Information Warfare Technical Center in Fort Meade, Maryland, has the right embryonic structure for the proposed ISAC. Such a facility, located within the structure of one of the world's most intrusive intelligence agencies, would constitute a grave threat to the privacy of not only law-abiding American citizens but citizens of other countries as well.

The Pentagon/NSA Angle

Congress has a "particular obligation to examine the NSA, in light of its tremendous potential for abuse. ... The danger lies in the ability of NSA to turn its awesome technology against domestic communications."

The Department of Defense and its secretive component, the NSA, were the driving forces behind critical infrastructure protection. They convinced the administration that it was necessary to defend the infrastructures of the United States in order to further offensive and defensive information warfare contingencies — notions partly drawn up by think tanks like the RAND Corporation and hyped by Hollywood screen writers. In fact, some computer experts interviewed by Reuters claimed the "threat is more Hollywood than hard fact." They added that some information security companies are using information warfare as a catalyst for more security software and gadgetry by exploiting the fear associated with a cyber-attack. The same phenomenon exists with the feared Year 2000 calamity.

For the Pentagon and the intelligence community, information warfare offered a new vista in an era of post-Cold War diminishing military budgets, paucity of conventional threats, base closures, and reductions in force of both military and civilian employees.

NSDD-145

The information security component of critical infrastructure protection - namely the withholding of what the government deems is "sensitive" information in the private sector - has roots in the Reagan administration. It is important to examine the policy decisions then in order to understand what is driving the current critical infrastructure and information warfare initiatives.

Responsibility for computer security standards within the civilian government had, until 1984, been assigned to the National Bureau of Standards (NBS). During the 1970s, NBS became a pivotal player in the development of computer security standards, particularly the widely accepted Data Encryption Standard (DES). The result of these developments was that NSA faced unprecedented competition from a civilian agency within the Department of Commerce in the area of encryption technology.

On September 17, 1984, NSA prevailed upon President Reagan to sign National Security Decision Directive 145 (NSDD-145). The directive authorized NSA to develop means to protect "unclassified sensitive" information. For the first time in its thirty-two year history, the NSA was assigned responsibilities outside its traditional foreign eavesdropping and military and diplomatic communications security roles.

The agency was granted new powers to curb the use of public cryptography and to develop standards and techniques for automated systems security. In addition, NSDD-145 permitted NSA to control the dissemination of government, government-derived, and even non-government information that might adversely affect the national security. Some argued that such a broad definition included *all* information. NSA quickly began to exercise its new-found authority.

The directive also stated that NSA was to act as the government's focal point for information security and as such was to:

> . . . review and approve *all* standards, techniques, systems and equipment for telecommunications and automated equipment security.

NSA also put pressure on the continued viability of DES when it announced that it would no longer certify DES products used by the government after 1988. Ignoring NBS's role within the civilian government agencies, NSA mandated the use of its own secretly-developed encryption algorithms - as part of a program called the Commercial COMSEC Endorsement Program or CCEP - by all government agencies. On November 5, 1986, National Security Adviser John Poindexter, who was embroiled in controversy stemming from the Iran-Contra scandal, further expanded NSA's information security role when he signed National Telecommunications and Information Systems Security Policy (NTISSP) Officially titled "Protection of Sensitive, But Unclassified Information in Federal Government Telecommunications and Automated Information Systems", Poindexter's directive extended NSA's mandate to the protection of unclassified sensitive information in the commercial data bases of private corporations. NSA found itself in charge of a program that was at variance with the Constitution and its Bill of Rights.

At about the same time, NSA began lobbying against two bills in Congress that were aimed at curtailing NSA's influence in the civilian government and commercial sectors. House Resolutions 2889 and 145 reinforced NBS's authority over the security civil government computer systems and networks by enshrining it in public law. National Computer Security Center director Patrick R. Gallagher, Jr., in a December 22, 1986 letter to Donald C. Latham, the Pentagon's Assistant Secretary of Defense for Command, Control, Communications, and Intelligence and the Chairman of the National Telecommunications and Information

Systems Security Committee (NTISSC), reported that his staff "provided support for [the] lobbying effort that successfully blocked HR 2889 from passage by the 99th Congress." NBS and certain members of Congress were eyeing NSA's computer security center, hoping to move it from NSA to NBS along with a budget approaching $1 billion. HR 145, also known as the Computer Security Act of 1987, ultimately fared better than HR 2889, but, it too, faced the same antagonistic NSA lobbying effort.

In testimony before the Chairman of the House Government Operations Committee in February 1987, the NSA director, General William Odom, was questioned on NSA congressional lobbying by the committee chairman Jack Brooks of Texas. Brooks asked Odom, "Did NSA officials contact private companies to gather support for NSA's opposition to HR 2889 or HR 145? If so, did you authorize these efforts?" Odom answered in writing that "NSA has no knowledge that any of its employees initiated contact with private companies for the purpose of gathering opposition support against HR 2889 or HR 145." Brooks' line of questioning was prompted by reported Congressional lobbying on NSA's behalf by officials and agents of one of its main computer security evaluation contractors, the MITRE Corporation, and by one of its major computer vendors, Digital Equipment Corporation (DEC).

In replying to a question from Representative Gerald Kleczka of Wisconsin on whether NSA staff members lobbied against the bill, Odom was a bit more forthcoming. He responded, "The answer is yes, sir. It's not the sense of the word that you used, ëlobby.' It's a sense of talking to Members of the Congress as we do on all sorts of legislation . . ."

> Brooks made it quite clear to General Odom what he thought of NSA's computer security lobbying efforts on the Hill when he asked the NSA chief, "Are you aware that it is illegal, against the law, for Government officials to use appropriated funds to lobby Congress on a piece of legislation? Odom replied, yes sir.

Most irksome for Brooks were official visits made by NSA, FBI, and CIA agents to U.S. companies that provided on-line access to computer databases. NSDD-145, in creating a new information category called "unclassified but sensitive," made commercial providers of such information subject to government security controls. One of the largest database providers visited by the government intelligence agents was Dialog, at the time the largest on-line vendor of data in the world. Dialog controlled around 270 databases that contained both commercial and government information.

Brooks then called Latham to testify. The chairman made known his feelings about NSDD 145:

> . . . one of the most ill-advised and potentially troublesome directives ever issued by a President. First, it was drafted in a manner, which usurps Congress's role in setting national policy.

Second, the directive is in conflict with existing statutes which assign to the Office of Management and Budget, the Department of Commerce, and the General Services Administration the sole responsibility for establishing government-wide standards, guidelines and policies for computer and telecommunications security.

Finally, seriously question the wisdom of the President's decision to give DOD the power to classify, hence control, information located in civilian agencies and even the private sector which, in DOD's opinion, may affect national security.

Latham, in his testimony, denied that he or anyone else in the NTISSC group had any plans to impose controls on unclassified information in the private sector. However, on November 11, 1986, six days after Admiral Poindexter issued his directive establishing the "unclassified but sensitive category," Diane Fountaine, Latham's Pentagon assistant, shocked a meeting of the Information Industry Association by confirming that the Reagan administration wanted to restrict access to public databases.

In fact, Latham was enforcing both NSDD-145 and the Poindexter Directive to the letter. In September 1986, this resulted in a visit by an NSA official to the headquarters of Mead Data Central in Columbus, Ohio. Mead operated two well-known repositories of data - NEXIS, a well-spring of news from the U.S. and foreign press, and LEXIS, a source data for court cites and other legal data.

The question is, how do you do that technically without interference?" NSA soon began investigating ways to eavesdrop on computer communications without being detected. The perfect method would be to use a computer program to surreptitiously monitor data base requests for particular categories of information. A user who would conduct a data base search using such keywords as "nuclear weapons", "stealth technology", or "National Security Agency" could activate such monitors, alerting the NSA about the database requests. For the NSA, the agency that had pioneered the development of text and voice keyword recognition systems, the monitoring of data base queries would not be an insurmountable task. Marc Rotenberg, the former counsel for Senator Patrick Leahy's Subcommittee on Technology and Law Senate (and present director of EPIC), later testified before the House Subcommittee on Legislation and National Security that NSA's visits to private companies "leaves open the possibility that any Federal agency could request that the NSA undertake an assessment of any information system maintained by a Federal contractor."

He urged the Congress to limit the authority of the NSA in computer security and to establish adequate means for public accountability. He also recommended in 1989 that Congress begin public hearings on the role of encryption technology in computer security. "Discussions about cryptography must become public discussions, regardless of the agencies involved."

Industry's Refusal to Cooperate

The NSA and Pentagon visitors to Mead Data Central were not only interested in stemming the flow of technical data to the Soviets and others, but also in trying to co-opt Mead to provide information on their Soviet bloc clients. Mead would have nothing to do with such a deal. Company president Jack W. Simpson refused to become a snitch for the intelligence community, declaring, "They would control GI Joe dolls as militarily significant if they could get away with it." Gerald Yung, Mead's general counsel, affirmed that "our clients are confidential." Lockheed Dialog's General Counsel Robert A. Simons broke with the Pentagon and NSA and questioned the government's activities: "Will we all need a passport to enter a public library?" Simons' boss,

Dialog President Roger Summit. said "I don't know under what authority it [control of private data bases] would be implemented." Likewise, Kenneth B. Allen, the vice president for government relations of the Information Industry Association, the trade group of commercial data base companies, criticized the administration's stance: "We think it is dangerous for the government to censor or restrict the flow of information," adding, "We're just looking at the opening salvos here." In light of the recent critical infrastructure and information warfare initiatives, Allen's words could not have been more prophetic.

The Computer Security Act

Despite the opposition of NSA and the Pentagon, Congress passed the Computer Security Act of 1987. The House Report on the legislation notes that NSDD 145 "raised considerable concern within the private sector and the Congress." One of the principal objections to the directive was that it gave NSA the authority to use its considerable foreign intelligence expertise within this country. This is particularly troubling since NSA was not created by Congress, but by a secret presidential directive and it has, on occasion, improperly targeted American citizens for surveillance.

Spurred to passage by Senators Patrick Leahy and Lawton Chiles and by Representatives Jack Brooks and Dan Glickman, Public Law 100-235 firmly established the role of the NBS (later renamed the National Institute of Standards and Technology or NIST) in establishing security standards for computer systems and networks processing unclassified information. But NSA still maintained a hook into the unclassified sector — one that it would begin to exploit to the maximum extent possible. The Computer Security Act called for NIST to draw on NSA for "technical assistance" in particular areas, especially cryptography.

In 1989, NSA and NIST signed a Memorandum of Understanding (MOU). The memorandum effectively returned to NSA many of the powers rejected by the Computer Security Act. The MOU contained several key goals that were to NSA's benefit, including: NSA providing NIST with "technical security guidelines in trusted technology, telecommunications security, and personal identification that may be used in cost-effective systems for protecting sensitive computer data;" NSA "initiating research and development programs in trusted technology, telecommunications security, cryptographic techniques and personal identification methods"; and NSA being responsive to NIST "in *all* matters related to cryptographic algorithms and cryptographic techniques including *but not limited to* research, development, evaluation, or endorsement."

The MOU was signed in March 1989 by Vice Admiral William O. Studeman, Odom's successor as NSA director, and Raymond G. Kammer, NIST's acting director and a disciple of NSA principles. NSA, once again, re-established its cryptographic hegemony within the government. Cynically, Studeman wrote a letter to Congressman John Conyers in June 1989 stating that it was NSA's "fondest desire . . . to work with NIST to start the momentum toward increased fielding of technology, standards, and guidelines in pursuit of PL 100-235 objectives."

The Clipper Conundrum

By early 1993, NSA was, once more, clearly in the driver's seat in protecting computerized information in the civil government sector. It, along with its allies in the Justice Department and FBI, sold the incoming Clinton administration on the technology of escrowed encryption. Most notable was the "Clipper Chip", a backdoor in digitized telephone scrambling programs that permitted law enforcement and intelligence agencies to listen in. The national firestorm that erupted forced many traditional NSA hidden agendas into public view, a situation which NSA found increasingly uncomfortable. NSA's escrowed encryption proposals, the FBI's "Digital Telephony" proposals to give it virtual real-time access to the nation's digital telecommunications network, and the Clinton administration's continuation of arcane "munitions" export controls on acceptable strength cryptography, continued into the critical infrastructure protection debate.

Within the business community, there is an underlying suspicion of government intentions, particularly in the computer and telecommunications industries. The privacy and civil liberties communities are inherently suspicious of administration intentions after witnessing a panoply of intrusive and anti-privacy measures being introduced in proposed legislation or by administrative fiat.

Clipper to Information Warfare

Control of cryptography is important to NSA but there is another area in which the agency has always wanted to stake a claim — computer intelligence. Throughout the late 1980s, a group of computer intruders operating out of Hannover, West Germany were discovered to be breaking into the computer systems of U.S. and foreign government agencies and corporations.

Furthermore, the hackers were found to be acting on behalf of the Soviet KGB. This incident gave NSA and other intelligence agencies the opportunity to expand their charters. In the spring of 1991, during Desert Storm operations in the Gulf, computer hackers from The Netherlands accessed U.S. military computers connected to the Internet. In all, some thirty-four DOD sites were penetrated according to the General Accounting Office (GAO).

In testimony before the Senate Subcommittee on Government Information and Regulation, GAO official Jack L. Brock, Jr. revealed that "at many of the sites, the hackers had access to unclassified, sensitive information." The use of the term "unclassified, sensitive information" was a windfall for NSA. It could confidently resurrect the tenets of NSDD-145 by arguing that it was necessary to protect such information, even though it was available via the publicly-accessible Internet.

NSA, however, still faced some wary members of Congress who were reluctant to expand NSA's powers in contravention of the Computer Security Act. In November 1991, Senator Herb Kohl, the chairman of the Senate subcommittee on Government Information and Regulation, sent a letter to Commerce Secretary Robert Mosbacher, in which he wrote that he held the Commerce Department, not NSA, responsible for the break-in by Dutch teenage hackers into the DOD computers containing "sensitive" information. Kohl also stated that "if the provisions of the Computer Security Act were followed these break-ins would be much less likely to happen." The senator urged Mosbacher to "make computer security a higher priority at the Department of Commerce."

Regardless of Kohl's stance, NSA was determined to take control of the protection of unclassified but sensitive information. In July 1994, NSA's new director, Vice Admiral Mike McConnell, wrote a letter to Senator Ernest Hollings, a key member of the Senate Appropriations Committee, declaring that "the threat to these [computer] systems is real . . . network/computer protection within DOD is a fundamental readiness issue and the need for security products is immediate."

But NSA was clearly looking for new reasons for existence. With the collapse of the Soviet Union, the Warsaw Pact, and a shrinking U.S. military budget, NSA's huge infrastructure and budget were being eyed by anxious budget-cutters. After the closure of NSA eavesdropping stations from Iceland to Alaska, NSA was clearly in search of an expanded mission that would supplement its signals intelligence and communications security responsibilities. Computer intelligence-gathering and computerized digital countermeasures were the answer. The term "information warfare" was coined and the NSA saw it as a natural area in which to assume responsibility.

By 1994, NSA positioned itself to become the top government information warfare-fighting agency. Because many government officials were not exactly sure what "information warfare" was, since no one had ever actually fought one, the Defense Department decided to come up with a definition. According to DOD, information warfare involves "actions taken to achieve information superiority in support of national military strategy by affecting adversary information and information systems while leveraging and protecting our own information and information systems."

NSA set about to influence the information warfare proposals that were being drawn up by a Defense Science Board information warfare panel that met during the summer of 1994. The panel's findings would have a great deal of influence on President Clinton's emerging information warfare policy doctrine. Fortunately for NSA, the information warfare panel of the study group was chaired by a former Reagan administration official, Donald Latham, who was then working for Loral Federal Systems, a large intelligence community contractor.

To consolidate its position, NSA approved the creation of the Defensive Information Warfare Program within the Defense Information Systems Agency (DISA) - a component of the Pentagon. By doing so, NSA was staking the same claim to "Infowar" that it had already established for "Infosec" within the DOD infrastructure. Information warfare also extended DOD's responsibilities in disseminating disinformation, a technique mastered by the KGB during the Cold War.

The significant impact of an information war on the international media is clear. Thomas Czerwinski, a professor at the School of Information Warfare and Strategy at the National Defense University in Washington, prophesied about an information war when he asked, "What would happen if you took Sadaam Hussein's image, altered it, and projected it back to Iraq showing him voicing doubts about his own Baath Party?" But the same technology could also be used to discredit democratically-elected leaders with whom the United States disagreed. DOD's move into the area of disinformation, morphing software, perception management, and censorship potentially pits its "cyber warriors" against the nation's "cyber libertarians."

War on Information

Charles Swett, a Pentagon official in the Office of the Assistant Secretary of Defense for Special Operations and Low Intensity Conflict, warned in 1995 that "the political process is moving on to the Internet." Swett charged that the Zapatista National Liberation Front was lying in their Internet communiqués in claiming the Mexican army had raped and killed children in Chiapas. Swett also argued that the Pentagon should begin scanning "left-wing" news on Internet sites in order to keep track of political activists operating domestically and abroad.

However, the Pentagon has a vested interest in trying to eliminate the Zapatista presence on the Internet. The U.S. Army's Special Forces have been involved in training Mexico's army in counter-insurgency operations against the Zapatistas, a group which has only been deemed terrorist by the Mexican oligarchy, New York banks and securities firms, and U.S. military and intelligence officials. In June 1995, then-CIA director John Deutch accused "terrorists" of using the Internet for their own communications. In addition, the Defense Intelligence Agency (DIA) maintains a list of 70 "rebel" Web sites.

Unfortunately, the DIA is involved in psychological warfare operations with several unsavory governments in helping them quell "rebel" movements. Many of these movements are considered "terrorist" only in the eyes of dictatorial regimes supported by the U.S. military. Freedom movements around the world, like the Zapatistas in Chiapas, the Tibetans, East Turkestanis, Bougainvilleans, Chechnians, West Papuans, Iranian Mojaheddin, Kurdistanis, Chinese democrats, and East Timorese, are using the Internet to communicate information about the horrific situation in their lands.

The Pentagon's information warriors have made a habit of confusing Internet activism by such groups with "cyber-attacks." For example, in May 1998, the U.S. information warfare structure announced that the Liberation Tigers of Tamil Eelam, a group fighting for independence from Sri Lanka, had successfully launched a cyber-terrorist assault on Sri Lankan computer systems. In reality, the attack was nothing more than a counter-propaganda e-mail flooding of Sri Lankan embassy web sites.

In an annual survey of terrorist incidents, the State Department charged a Tamil group called the Internet Black Tigers with "suicide e-mail bombings" of Sri Lankan web sites. The Tamil group, far from engaging in anything so dramatic, was merely trying to counter Sri Lankan propaganda directed against the Tamils. Using the Pentagon's and State Department's lexicology, one could equate the posting of anti-government banners and posters on a government building as a form of terrorism. Many experts scoff at the notion that the Internet is vulnerable to terrorist attack. According to Neil Barrett, a principal consultant of Europe's Groupe Bull, "terrorist groups are not using the Internet for anything more than propaganda and internal communications." Barrett also stated that there is a lot of exaggeration over what constitutes a cyber terrorist attack. He cited one case in which an Internet chess club web site was attacked by hackers — the intrusion was later described as a terrorist attack.

Similarly, when the Pentagon alleged that its computer systems were subjected to 250,000 hacker intrusions, it failed to mention that all but 500 of these were mere Internet "pings", a sort of inquiry that can be generated by a search engine looking for information on "nuclear weapons", "missiles", or "chemical warfare", all subjects that would be contained in the Pentagon's Internet-connected systems. However, such search engine "pings" hardly constitute cyber-terrorist attacks.

The Congress should consider measures aimed at preventing the U.S. military and intelligence community, particularly the CIA, DIA, FBI, and NSA from engaging in activities aimed at disrupting the free flow of human rights information on the Internet. Specifically, Internet intelligence-sharing between the United States and nations that violate human rights should be strictly restricted.

The information warfare proponents also seek to spread disinformation via the Internet. The Pentagon and intelligence community have traditionally used such tactics as "spoofing" the airwaves with false messages and distributing propaganda through television and radio broadcasts, air dropping of leaflets, and planting of false stories in foreign newspapers and magazines. For example, the U.S. Air Force Special Operations Command maintains six EC-130 aircraft (code-named Commando Solo) that are designed to broadcast propaganda to civilians over AM, FM, shortwave, and television frequencies. These aircraft have been used in military operations in Saudi Arabia, Turkey, Bosnia, Haiti, Panama, and Grenada. In addition, U.S. Army psychological operations propaganda specialists publish the weekly *Herald of Peace* newspaper in both Serbian and Croatian, which is distributed throughout Bosnia. The Pentagon planners feel that if another country or group resists U.S. policy they are fair game for a propaganda assault. In a paper written for the U.S.

Air University, U.S. Air Force Colonel Richard Szafranski maintains that "Information warfare is hostile activity directed against any part of the knowledge and belief systems of an adversary." The use of the Internet for similar disinformation and propagandizing during peacetime could potentially violate laws and U.S. Information Agency regulations intended to shield American citizens from such manipulation and deception. These laws and regulations should be revisited by Congress in consideration of future critical infrastructure protection appropriations.

Info-Warriors

NSA has put its service cryptologic elements to work on information warfare. The Army got a head start in 1990 when its Signal Warfare Center at Vint Hill Farms, Virginia began soliciting companies to propose the development of destructive computer viruses, self-reproducing malicious computer instructions contained in computer memory that can, if properly programmed, destroy information stored in a computer. The Army, a pioneer in the development of deadly biological viruses at its Fort Detrick, Maryland germ warfare facility, was interested in developing surreptitious programs to launch at an enemy's computer systems and networks, perhaps transmitting destructive computer codes by radio. Computer security specialists warned that such research could potentially backfire against a computer aggressor. Many reasoned that the United States was more vulnerable to the potential "bounce back" effect of such viruses. Nevertheless, NSA's military components began to ready their computer terminals for information warfare. For example, the Army created its information warfare center at Fort Belvoir, Virginia. Known as the Land Information Warfare Activity (LIWA), it is co-located with the Army Intelligence and Security Command, the Army component of NSA's Central Security Service (CSS). According to a LIWA spokesperson, the Army is "looking beyond the land battle with information warfare initiatives and new technology."

In 1996, the Air Force established its Information Warfare Center at Kelly Air Force Base, Texas. This activity is co-located with the Air Intelligence Agency, the Air Force component of NSA's CSS, and the NSA's Medina Annex Regional Signals Intelligence (SIGINT) Operations Center (RSOC).

The Naval Information Warfare Activity at Fort Meade, Maryland, is located with the Naval Security Group Command, the Navy component of the NSA's CSS. In addition, the Navy's Fleet Information Warfare at the Navy's Atlantic Fleet headquarters in Norfolk, Virginia, is developing new methods for information warfare.

Armed with a new mission of defending against a cyber-attack, NSA further eroded the provisions of the Computer Security Act by offering its services to numerous federal agencies, including the Department of Interior, National Aeronautics and Space Administration, and the Department of the Treasury. For example, NSA penetration teams tried to access unclassified computer networks at NASA to probe the vulnerabilities of satellite control, launch control and other operations. Even more alarming was the fact that the General Accounting Office (GAO), the congressional watchdog agency that is tasked with ensuring federal agencies are complying with laws like the Computer Security Act, asked NSA to conduct the penetration testing of NASA, an agency which clearly falls under the purview of NIST.

The intelligence community and Pentagon also ensured a body of congressional champions of information warfare advocates and supporters. Chief among them are Senator Jon Kyl, whose Subcommittee on Technology, Terrorism, and Government Information has held numerous hearings featuring "gloom and doom" witnesses complaining that the nation is one the verge of an "electronic Pearl Harbor" and even more distastefully, an "electronic Oklahoma City."

The PCCIP, contains a number of proposals that could, if implemented, adversely affect the freedom of American citizens. Many of the proposals affecting the ability of Americans to engage in scientific and other research, as well as political and social discourse, without being subjected to government security controls, are a direct outgrowth of similar proposals advanced by President Reagan's NSDD-145.

Privacy

The PCCIP, complains that because private sector

employers do not have access to criminal history, financial, and employment information and also may incur tort liability for releasing adverse employment information to other employers, the private sector should be granted limited exemptions from these restrictions. The Report recommends that federal and state laws be amended to "balance employers' needs against individual interests in privacy." Such a recommendation is frightening in light of reports that companies are increasingly monitoring the communications of their employees.

The degree to which companies may be required or encouraged to hand over the contents of such communications to the FBI's National Infrastructure Threat Center also poses significant civil liberties concerns. Many companies currently possess and use monitoring capabilities. A MacWorld survey revealed that 22 per cent of large companies "engaged in searches of employee computer files, voice mail, electronic mail, or other networking communications." Only one-third of these companies informed employees that such surveillance was taking place.

A 1997 survey by the American Management Association showed that more than 35 per cent of employers use surveillance tactics such as reviewing e-mail, inspecting computer files, or eavesdropping on phone conversations. The Report also recommends that state legislators amend their privacy laws to require mere implied "consent" as authority for employers to request sensitive background information on employees or prospective employees. In addition, there is a recommendation that Congress amend the Employee Polygraph Protection Act to include information security personnel in the category of professions which can be required to be subjected to polygraph tests.

Freedom of Information, Open Government, and Censorship

The PCCIP Report recommends that the Critical Infrastructure Assurance Office (CIAO) established by PDD-63 require appropriate protection for specified private sector information. It, therefore, proposes to require that the Freedom of Information Act (FOIA) exemptions of paragraph b (3) be broadened to include "sensitive information" from the private sector.

At a partially-open meeting of the Advisory Committee to PCCIP held on December 3, 1997, Steve Mitchell from the Justice Department called for a "cultural change" to take place over the next 15 to 20 years in order to deal with the information warfare threat. He called for FOIA exemptions under both Federal and state law for companies passing on proprietary information to government agencies. He also said state FOIAs, in particular, should be amended because they are often more liberal than the Federal law on opening up government documents and files to the public. Mitchell also called for some form of Federal Advisory Committee Act (FACA) relief for joint government-private sector boards and committees. He said this would permit sensitive but unclassified meetings to be closed to the public.

Another aspect of information warfare involves censorship and disinformation. According to a report written for the Pentagon by SAIC, "widespread dissemination by the U.S. media and its independence vastly complicate military operations. Any information warfare strategy must taken into account the press or *at least* address its potential impact."

Former NSA director and CIA deputy director Studeman stated that there should be a "rapid media reaction force" charged with disseminating propaganda to various media channels and outlets for "positive purposes". Studeman is currently the Vice President and Deputy General Manager of TRW's Systems and Information Technology Group, another contractor with a vested interest in critical infrastructure protection. Studeman also serves on the Board of Directors of Thiokol Corporation, formerly headed by PCCIP Commission Chairman Marsh.

Congress should ensure that the FOIA and FACA are not amended in any way that would inhibit the public's right to access unclassified information held by the government, regardless of the information's origin.

New Security Classification Category

The PCCIP Report recommends that the CIAO classify new categories of information such as "aggregated" unclassified information. It also recommends that the President use his Executive Order fiat authority to require federal agencies to identify purposes for publishing certain information and "ensure the information is published in a format that minimizes the likelihood it will be used in ways that are incompatible with infrastructure assurance." Creating new classification categories and restricting the dissemination of certain unclassified information to the public was a cornerstone of NSDD-145 and was rejected by the

Congress. In March 1997, the Commission on Protection and Reduction of Government Secrecy, headed by Senator Patrick Moynihan, concluded that there is too much classified information held by the federal government. Instead of calling for an expansion in the ability of federal agencies to classify information, as called for by the Marsh Commission, the Moynihan Commission recommended legislation to establish principles on what information can be classified, determine what information should not be classified, specify how long information should remain classified, and create a national declassification center to provide annual reports on the progress in declassifying government records.

In April 1997, after the issuance of the Moynihan Commission report, President Clinton stated, "I think there is too much secrecy in the government and I think too many people have too much unfettered discretion just to declare documents secret." The actions taken by President Clinton and the PCCIP to facilitate the establishment of new categories of "unclassified sensitive" and "aggregated sensitive" information are clearly at variance with the President's own public comments on limiting government secrecy. The administration should institute policies that are designed to limit the ability of agencies to classify documents, not extend such authority as called for in the PCCIP Report.

Internet Monitoring and Surveillance

In its Information Warfare (Defense) Report to the Undersecretary of Defense, the Defense Science Board (DSB) calls current technology to monitor the National

Information Infrastructure (NII) inadequate. The report recommends that an "investment" be made in developing a distributed monitoring and surveillance strategy for large scale networks. Large scale intelligence agency and law enforcement monitoring of the Internet is also suggested in the DSB report. Specifically, the report states "The Internet provides potential for access to rich repositories of open source information."

It further states that there are constitutional impediments to using the Internet for espionage: "IC (Intelligence Community) access to the Internet raises difficult questions and serious concerns about conflicts between law enforcement, intelligence activities, and constitutional guarantees." In the debate over the mandatory use of escrowed encryption, the balance between government access to decrypted data and privacy rights - something the Clinton administration calls "equities" - always appeared to favor access over privacy rights.

The DSB report seems to suggest that a similar "equity" situation exists with regard to espionage on the Internet. If past administration balances are considered, it would appear that intelligence and law enforcement espionage on the Internet outweighs the requirement to maintain constitutional guarantees. The Electronic Communications Privacy Act of 1986 should be strengthened to restrict massive government-led or government-inspired Internet surveillance in the name of "infrastructure assurance."

Encryption

The mandatory use of escrowed encryption/key recovery

technology is an inherent part of the current critical infrastructure protection proposals. The PCCIP Report states that "establishment of trustworthy key management infrastructures (KMIs) is the only way to enable encryption on a large scale."

Arguing for government access to encryption keys, the Report states, "key recovery is needed to provide business access to data when encryption keys are lost or maliciously misplaced, and court-authorized law enforcement access to the plain text of criminal-related communications and data lawfully seized." The Report also calls on the federal government to encourage efforts by commercial vendors to develop key recovery concepts and techniques.

Wells reaffirmed this when he said that DOD was "putting its money where its mouth is by requiring private vendors to turn over to DOD the encryption key to software programs enabling access to companies' encryption codes in the event of an emergency." By using the DOD officials as the chief proponents for key recovery schemes, the administration seeks to bring the debate under such rubrics as "critical infrastructure protection" and "homeland defense." One sector of the infrastructure that the PCCIP spent time looking into is the emergency services sector (police, fire, emergency medical services). However, according to a U.S. Department of Commerce memorandum from William A. Reinsch, the Undersecretary of Commerce for Export Administration, because key escrow products have a significant performance flaw, police forces in the United States and abroad are reluctant to use such products. The Reinsch memo points out that "police forces are reluctant to use ëescrowed' encryption products (such as radios in patrol cars). They are more costly and less efficient than non-escrowed products. There can be long gaps in reception due to the escrow features - sometimes as long as a ten-second pause. Our own police do not use recoverable encryption products; they buy the same non-escrowable products used by their counterparts in Europe and Japan.

Other government agencies may also reject key recovery — for example, some U.S. exports were to support Allied government agencies with signals intelligence missions similar to NSA's." Consequently, according to Reinsch, the performance flaws caused by key escrow would place such technology in the category of a threat to the emergency services and intelligence warning sectors of the critical infrastructure and not as a safeguard. Therefore, the administration should reconsider the use of key escrow/recovery technology as a component of critical infrastructure protection.

The Posse Comitatus Act

Congress passed the Posse Comitatus Act of 1878 (20 Stat. 152 [18 USC 1385]) in order to curb the military's role in law enforcement in the South. The act, as amended, states:

> Whosoever, except in cases and under circumstances expressly authorized by the Constitution or Act of Congress, willfully uses any part of the Army or the Air Force as a posse comitatus or otherwise to execute the laws shall be fined not more than $10,000 or imprisoned not more than two years, or both.

The DSB Report suggests that the Defense Department defend non-military computer systems. Such a suggestion runs afoul of both the Posse Comitatus Act and the Computer Security Act. The Report states:

> The SECDEF/DEPSECDEF should also task the General Counsel to propose legislation, regulation, or executive orders as may be needed to make clear the DOD role in defending non-DOD systems. This should specifically address the need for changes to the Computer Security Act, the capture of information on unidentified intruders (issue of intelligence collection on U.S. persons), the authority to conduct "hot pursuit" of intruders, and the ability to obtain reports from the operators of critical elements of the civil infrastructure.

Congress should revisit the provisions of the Posse Comitatus Act and ensure that the U.S. military is not permitted to engage in unwarranted intrusions into the privacy of U.S. citizens, as it did during the 1970s in monitoring the lawful activities of anti-Vietnam War protesters. Senator Charles Grassley of Iowa, the chairman of Judiciary Subcommittee on Administrative Oversight and the Courts, should be supported in his efforts to enforce the provisions of Posse Comitatus. In early 1997, when Senator Grassley discovered U.S. Army Colonel John Ellis was serving as deputy chief of the FBI's Domestic Terrorism Planning Section, he said, "to the extent we allow a Colonel Ellis incident to succeed, it confirms the militarization of law enforcement." Grassley added, "there should be a clear line of demarcation between the military and law enforcement. And I'm incensed because the people at the FBI and Justice are too stupid to see that."

Role for the FBI

The FBI played a large role in critical infrastructure

protection even before President Clinton signed PDD 62 and 63. It hosted two groups involved in infrastructure protection: the former CIITAC (Computer Investigation and Infrastructure Threat Assessment Center), and the interim Infrastructure Protection Task Force. Both were located at FBI headquarters. Of particular concern is the role the FBI has played in lobbying the legislative and judicial branches on its surveillance agenda. Such lobbying is reminiscent of that done by the NSA when it was trying to advance the agendas contained in NSDD-145 and stall the passage of the Computer Security Act. This resulted in a sharp rebuke from Representative Brooks who drew attention to the criminal provisions of Title 18, U.S.C. 1913. FBI Director Freeh's congressional lobbying efforts have been directed towards certain key members of the Senate, including Senators Phil Gramm, Orrin Hatch, Joseph Biden, Arlen Specter, and Patrick Leahy.

During 1981, Freeh, while serving as an FBI special agent, helped Senator Sam Nunn's Permanent Subcommittee on Investigations. Not coincidentally, Nunn, both during his time as senator and as co-chair of the PCCIP Advisory Committee, became a strong proponent of the administration's critical infrastructure proposals. It is also reported that the FBI's Office of Public and Congressional Affairs has grown to 85 full-time positions, becoming "one of the most effective lobbying operations in Washington, public or private."

Also troubling has been the FBI's lobbying directed at members of the federal judiciary. On July 15, 1998, Judge Royce Lamberth of the U.S. District Court for the District of Columbia and the chief judge of the secretive Foreign Intelligence Surveillance Court (FISC) — the court empowered to grant the NSA and FBI authority to conduct domestic wiretaps in cases involving national security — revealed that Freeh had been lobbying the judicial branch of the government for an international mandatory key recovery scheme. Freeh's lobbying efforts were conducted through the auspices of the Judicial Conference, the policy-making body for the Administrative Office of the US Courts. In one case, Freeh gave Lamberth and the six other members of the FISC a demonstration of what occurs when the FBI intercepts encrypted communications.

Lamberth said he was also convinced of the government's claims that it "takes trillions of years [for the government] to break encryption." According to Lamberth, Freeh was accompanied in his judicial lobbying visit by General John Gordon, representing CIA director George Tenet, and NSA director Lt. Gen. Kenneth Minihan. The blueprint for the FBI's expanding powers can be found in Vice President Gore's National Performance Review, issued on September 7, 1993. In it, Gore proposed:

> ... to integrate drug enforcement efforts of the DEA [Drug Enforcement Administration] and FBI. This will create savings in administrative and support functions such as laboratories, legal services, training facilities, and administration. Most important, the federal government will get a much more powerful weapon in its fight against crime.
>
> When this has been successfully accomplished, we will move toward combining the enforcement functions of the Bureau of Alcohol, Tobacco and Firearms (BATF) into the FBI . . ..

In granting the FBI widened powers to protect the critical infrastructure, particularly computers and networks, it is important to reflect on a comment by Representative Robert Barr of Georgia, himself a former U.S. attorney. He stated, "Federal law enforcement power far outweighs accountability." In 1997, the FBI was armed with new guidelines to investigate U.S. citizens suspected of supporting foreign groups deemed by the Secretary of State to be involved in terrorism. One result of this was the FBI's proposed "Bay Area Counterterrorism Task Force," which would combine the resources of the FBI, the Immigration and Naturalization Service, and the San Francisco Police Department to investigate Bay Area organizations, even if there were no grounds to suspect criminal activity.

The FBI's political surveillance efforts also conflict with San Francisco Police Department policy, which requires a special review before it can investigate crimes linked to political activity. According to a San Francisco Police Department memo, similar FBI programs exist in Chicago, Los Angeles, Boston, and Washington, D.C. The anxieties expressed by Senator Grassley and Representative Barr, as well as other legislators, should be transformed into legislation restricting the FBI, other law enforcement agencies, and intelligence agencies from engaging in domestic fishing expeditions aimed against U.S. citizens exercising their First Amendment rights.

Antitrust

The PCCIP Report recommends that the Department of Justice provide antitrust relief to certain private companies to enable them to jointly share information with the government. On July 15, 1998, an official of the NSA told Commerce Undersecretary Reinsch that NSA was trying to engage Microsoft and Intel in its critical infrastructure "solution" but did not want to run afoul of anti-trust laws. Promoting anti-trust relief in the name of protecting against nebulous futuristic information warfare threats appears to be a case of overreaction. Additionally, such anti-trust relief in an era of several mega-mergers between telecommunications giants calls into question the propriety of extending anti-trust exemptions to such a select group of corporations. Congress should ensure that anti-trust legislation is not weakened to facilitate infrastructure protection or information warfare initiatives.

Liability

The PCCIP Report recommends that the government examine liability relief for private corporations that share sensitive information with the federal government. This could include giving corporations immunity from law suits arising from invasions of employee and customer privacy, workplace-related injuries and sickness, environmental pollution, and internal fraud. Congress should enact legislation prohibiting the federal government from granting liability relief to companies that share sensitive information, where that sharing results in adverse employment actions being taken against individuals engaged in legal activities.

National Security and Foreign Corporations

The PCCIP Report recommends that the NSC establish standards for sharing critical infrastructure information with foreign corporations and the U.S. subsidiaries of foreign corporations. This places American-owned companies in a strategically better position to compete in the international marketplace and may be in violation of international free trade treaties to which the United States is a party.

State Government Liability

The PCCIP Report bemoans the fact that the number of diverse state laws complicates the maximization of information sharing with the federal government. It recommends that a study group be formed to re-draft state legislation to permit such information sharing. Chief targets of the federal government are the state privacy and freedom of information laws as well as numerous sectoral laws dealing with particular disclosures of confidential information, such as criminal justice records; bank records; credit information; employment records; library records; medical records; privileged communications with psychologists, clergymen, speech pathologists and audiologists, attorneys, accountants, and pharmacists; school records; and tax records.

Federal attempts to curtail state privacy laws should be resisted by federal legislation prohibiting the federal government from pre-empting state privacy laws. In addition, some state laws permit access to documents held by organizations not covered by the Federal FOIA. Federal attempts to limit disclosures at the state level will further erode a citizen's right to access public information. This should also be addressed in new federal legislation.

The PCCIP report recommends that the federal government - namely NSA, NIST, and the Department of

Education - work with private industry to develop a training program for information assurance specialists. The DOD's Linton Wells spoke of a Pentagon plan to create a GI-Bill type program to train computer security professionals. The DSB Report suggests loaning DOD personnel to the civil government and private sector to improve infrastructure protections.

The DSB also recommends that a "closed community" of experts of information warfare experts be established, and that a warning center be set up that would have the authority to mandate the reporting of all suspected intrusions and computer incidents affecting "DOD systems and networks" (now defined as any which could have an impact on the critical infrastructure). The PCCIP Report suggests providing monetary reward and payment-for-information programs to encourage on-line users to provide information on suspected computer crimes. Considering the fact that there already exists a number of professional certification programs in the private sector encompassing such disciplines as information systems security, internal auditing, data processing, computer programming, and network and system administration, proposals to create a virtual "cyber Stasi" of informants and federal deputies is offensive and should be deleted from all federal budget line items.

11

Rights to Privacy on Net

Internet communication is highly vulnerable to surveillance and interception. A government agency can violate the privacy of e-mail correspondence just as easily as it can tap a person's telephone in order to listen to conversations or intercept faxes. The equipment needed is neither costly nor complicated to operate. Authorities can monitor by tapping an individual phone line and intercepting data streams as they are sent and received. If a user has Internet access via a private ISP, employees of that ISP can open and read e-mail sent through it or allow police investigators to do so, unless special safeguards are put in place to protect privacy. If authorities have access to an ISP's server or the country's telecommunications network, they can capture e-mails while they are in transit.

Authorities can read, block, or delete messages based on such criteria as the e-mail address of the sender or the recipient, the Internet Protocol addresses identifying the sending computer and the destination computer(s), or the presence of specified character strings in the body of the message--say, the words "Emir" and "corruption" in close proximity. Such a system is analogous to a postal delivery system in which all pieces of mail are first delivered to a single location, where officials can inspect items at will.

Although data is broken up and sent in "packets," each packet contains Internet Protocol (IP) addresses. Packets can easily be reassembled while en route with the aid of eavesdropping tools.

An eavesdropper can generally identify the computer terminal that is sending or receiving data, but not the person who is typing on its keyboard. For this reason, some governments are uneasy about allowing computer terminals with Internet access in places where extra effort would be required to monitor who is using each terminal, for what, and when. A contract provided by Tunisia's state-run Agence Tunisienne d'Internet (ATI) requires institutional Internet subscribers to refrain from offering anyone remote access via their computers without prior authorization, and to declare to the ATI the names of all persons having accounts on, or access to, the computers and to inform the agency of changes in the user list.

Expression via the Internet includes the use of means that are private and others that are public. E-mail is private in the sense that the sender specifies the persons and addresses to whom it will be sent. (Of course, recipients can then re-send it to others or post it on a bulletin board, just as they can do with an ordinary letter.) By contrast, launching an open-access web site or posting a comment in a public newsgroup are acts of public speech since they are viewable by anyone who wishes to visit the web site or newsgroup.

Computer users have various means to protect their privacy and anonymity, some more effective than others. At the low-tech end, a user can try to avoid surveillance by using a computer terminal or e-mail account that is not being monitored, for example, one belonging to a friend. These techniques may help users escape identification if they are not already under surveillance, but they are no insurance against interception if a user's computer communication is being monitored.

Experts agree that there are basically three methods that, for the time being at least, make surveillance extremely difficult: direct-to-satellite and other forms of wireless transmission, anonymous re-mailers, and encryption.

Small dishes are available that enable users to transmit and receive data directly via satellite, bypassing the ground-based telecommunication system. These fit into a suitcase-sized carrying case and can be placed discreetly on a balcony while in use. They resemble in size the "pizza" dishes used to download satellite television broadcasts, but are capable of sending as well as receiving. Some countries of the Middle East and North Africa either ban or require permits for direct-to-satellite dishes. Cost also puts this technology beyond the reach of most individuals and nongovernmental organizations in the region. But as they grow more affordable and widespread, wireless communications offer a potent means of evading government monitoring and censorship.

Encryption, on the other hand, costs nothing or next to nothing. Strong and easy-to-use encryption software, such as the "Pretty Good Privacy" (PGP) program, can be downloaded for free from the World Wide Web and stored on a laptop or personal computer. While experts using powerful computers have been able to break strong encryption codes, the process requires considerable resources and time and is impractical for routine monitoring. Users should nevertheless pay attention to developments in the field--as well as to local laws governing the use of encryption. The Global Internet Liberty Campaign maintains a country-by-country review of legislation.

The right to encrypt messages is of particular importance to the protection of human rights. In many countries human rights organizations use PGP to protect the identity of witnesses and victims when sending data electronically. Rights groups in Guatemala, Ethiopia, Haiti, Mexico, South Africa, Hong Kong, and Turkey are among those that use encryption, according the GILC survey. Some groups use cryptographic techniques to digitally sign messages that they send over the Internet to ensure their integrity and authenticity, that is, to prove the messages are indeed coming from them and have not been altered in transmission.

The power of encryption to foil monitoring has led a number of governments to impose restrictions on the use, sale, and export of encryption software. Tunisia, Saudi Arabia, and Israel are among those countries that ban the use of encryption without prior authorization.

Encryption has an Achilles heel: it may effectively shield a message's contents from an eavesdropper but not the fact that something has been encoded. This alone may lead to harsh consequences if the authorities wish to punish the sender or recipient, or coerce them to disclose the message's contents or their "private keys." Upon obtaining the latter, authorities could then read every message encrypted with the user's "public key" or use the compromised private key to impersonate that user in corresponding with others.

One way to circumvent this danger is to camouflage encrypted messages by using steganography. This type of program hides one form of data inside another—for example, text inside a graphic image or a video or audio clip--in such a way that makes it more likely to escape detection by interlopers. For example, a sensitive document proving that a police unit moonlighted as a death squad can be encrypted and embedded in a photograph of a soccer team, and then e-mailed to a person outside the country who has the means to extract the document. Steganography software can be downloaded for free from the World Wide Web. However, some experts warn that sophisticated eavesdroppers can detect when a file has something steganographically hidden in it.

The third anti-surveillance strategy is to route communications via secure and trusted web-based re-mailing services that forward them to the designated recipient only after expunging the original address and other identifying data. To reduce traceability further, users can select re-mailers that keep no records of the addresses from which they receive, and to which they send, data. They can also program messages to pass through more than one re-mailer; some re-mailers do this automatically. And if their browser supports strong encryption, they can choose a re-mailer that encrypts all messages as they are sent to that re-mailer, which then sends them on to the intended recipient in decrypted form. In the latter scenario, even if an eavesdropper is "sniffing" a person's Internet activities, the eavesdropper can at most discern that the person is visiting a particular web site but not the content of the messages that the person is sending, the intended recipients, or whether the person has encrypted messages before sending them. For obvious reasons, some governments see anonymizing re-mailers as undesirable and have blocked them.

Another potential problem with anonymizers is that they do not guarantee that the user's identity will remain unknown to the anonymizing service itself or to the user's ISP. Researcher are addressing this concern. One tool that is still in prototype form is "Crowds." It works by collecting Web users into a geographically diverse group that performs Web transactions on behalf of its individual members in a way that prevents Web servers, other "crowd" members, and eavesdroppers from identifying the sender of a particular communication.

12

Right to Free Expression

Government-imposed filtering poses two basic threats to the right to free expression. First, as explained in the legal section above, it constitutes a form of prior censorship and as such should be subjected to the strictest level of scrutiny. Second, in practical terms, the filtering technologies developed so far are imprecise tools. Even when the stated motives for content-filtering have been justifiable, such as to keep pornographic materials from minors, the means used have almost invariably impeded, whether intentionally or not, the flow of political, cultural, medical and other types of content that are unquestionably legal under international standards.

In Bahrain, Iran, Saudi Arabia, the United Arab Emirates, and Yemen, ISPs--either under government orders or pressure--all block web sites on the basis of their content. In the first four if not all of these countries, blocking extends to cultural and/or political content.

U.A.E. officials are perhaps more forthcoming than others that engage in blocking. They justify it as a means of limiting access to pornography. Persons in the Emirates who dial up a local service provider do not have unmediated access to the Internet. Rather, their requests are routed through a proxy server maintained by the government-controlled telecommunications company, Etisalat. When a user requests a web site, the request will be refused if the filtering software on the proxy server detects "objectionable" material on the site or finds that the site is on a list of banned sites. The presence on the U.A.E.'s list of taboo sites of a political and cultural web site for Arab homosexuals refutes official claims that only pornography is banned.

A proxy server such as the ones in place in the U.A.E. and Saudi Arabia can be used by authorities to track which computer terminals are accessing which web sites and for how long. U.A.E. authorities deny monitoring individual web use. In Saudi Arabia, however, users who request a site that is blocked get a message on their screens warning that all access attempts are logged.

State-controlled or state-influenced Internet Service Providers in Tunisia, Iran, and Bahrain block web sites containing political or human rights criticism of the government. Tunisia has acknowledged blocking only those sites that offend moral values, but apparently this includes the sites of various human rights organizations critical of the government.

Bahrain has been less aggressive than neighboring Saudi Arabia and the U.A.E. in trying to block pornography centrally. Although there are reports that it is blocking some sexually explicit sites, Batelco, the state-controlled monopoly service provider, seems to rely more on encouraging subscribers to download filtering programs, should they desire it.

The ability of minors to access online pornography was one impetus for the enactment in 1996 by the U.S. Congress of the Communications Decency Act (CDA). The act criminalized online communication that is "obscene, lewd, lascivious, filthy, or indecent, with intent to annoy, abuse, threaten, or harass another person," or "obscene or indecent" if the recipient of the communication is under eighteen years of age.

The CDA was opposed by a coalition of human rights and free expression groups. As Human Rights Watch, a member group of the coalition, argued in an affidavit to the Supreme Court, the law's prohibition of "indecent" speech could be applied to its own human rights reporting that includes graphic accounts of rape and other forms of sexual abuse. In an important ruling for Internet liberties, the U.S. Supreme Court in 1997 voided key provisions of the act on the grounds that the Internet is entitled to the highest level of free speech protection and the act violated that principle.

While cautioning that all methods of controlling access to Internet content pose dangers to the right to impart and receive information, some international civil liberties organizations have argued that filtering software installed by the end-user raises fewer freedom-of-speech concerns than censorship imposed from above.

Filtering software works by examining a data stream and blocking any material that matches specified criteria, such as the presence of "stop words" in a web site's home page or URL, or the presence of the URL on a list of banned sites A more aggressive type of software, such as the KidDesk Internet Safe program, "white-lists" material by prohibiting access to all materials except those that are explicitly approved by the parent or supervisor.

Making the case that end-user filtering software is preferable to government censorship, the Center for Democracy and Technology, a Washington, D.C.-based organization, argues:

> By placing control over content in the hands of individual parents, as opposed to bureaucrats and prosecutors, policy makers can assure full respect for our constitutional protection of freedom of expression and enable the Internet to grow free from unnecessary and ineffective regulatory interference....A great variety of blocking and filtering software exists which can serve the diversity of family values of American communities, providing choice to families online without infringing the constitutional First Amendment rights of Internet users.

Whether employed by end-users or government servers, filtering software is an imprecise tool that in practice almost always blocks materials beyond its stated purpose. This is true even of the more sophisticated products that are regularly updated by staff members who check web sites for "suitability." According to popular anecdotes, software that hunted for specified "stop words" ended up blocking sites that mentioned the English county of Middlesex and recipes for chicken breasts. One popular program blocked a web site containing information on AIDS prevention. Even a pro-filtering web site was once blocked by Surf Watch, a leading filtering program, because it shared a commercial server with a pornographic site.

13

Information Security

The need to protect sensitive and critical federal data has been recognized for years in various laws, including the Privacy Act of 1974; the Paperwork Reduction Act of 1980, as amended; and the Computer Security Act of 1987. However, information security has taken on new significance as both reliance on computers and vulnerabilities associated with networked systems have increased. This is because the same techniques that agencies are employing to help cut costs and improve service—interconnected systems, readily accessible information, and paperless processing—are also factors that increase the vulnerability of operations and data to unauthorized modification and disclosure and to potentially devastating interruptions in service. Agency managers have the primary responsibility for ensuring the security of their information resources, and they are in the best position to assess the risks associated with their programs and to develop and implement policies to mitigate these risks. However, since enactment of the original Paperwork Reduction Act in 1980, OMB has been responsible for developing government wide guidance on information security and overseeing agency practices. Because of the breadth, significance, and complexity of this oversight challenge, it is important that OMB develop all possible strategies and assets—especially processes, staff expertise, and relevant information—to support its relatively small staff in fulfilling this responsibility.

Over the past 4 years, GAO has issued over 30 reports describing serious information security problems at major federal agencies, and agency inspectors general have issued numerous others. Our analysis of the most recent of these reports for the 15 largest federal agencies found that 10 agencies had serious information security weaknesses, some of which have existed for years. Material weaknesses were not reported for the other five agencies. However, independent reviews of computer-related controls at three of these five agencies were either not performed or were very limited.

The most common problems reported were (1) poor controls over access to sensitive and critical data and (2) incomplete and untested disaster recovery plans—weaknesses that essentially preclude an agency from reasonably ensuring the integrity, confidentiality, and availability of critical and sensitive computerized data, such as tax payer information and federal financial records. Examples include the following:

— Estimates by the Department of Defense indicate that attacks on unclassified computer systems and networks are a serious and growing threat to our national security, including Defense's ability to execute military operations and protect sensitive information. Defense data indicate that Defense may have experienced as many as 250,000 attacks in 1995 and that the number of attacks is doubling each year. Successful attacks by outside intruders have shut down systems and corrupted sensitive data. However, estimates based on tests conducted since 1992 showed that less than 1 percent of attacks on Defense's systems were detected and reported. Although no summary costs have been developed, Defense officials estimate that the cost of such incidents is at least tens of millions of dollars per year.

— Annual audits since 1993 have found that due to poor computer controls, IRS cannot ensure that the confidentiality and accuracy of taxpayer data are protected and that the data are not manipulated for purposes of individual gain. Specifically, controls have not prevented users from unauthorized access to sensitive programs and data files, numerous users have been allowed powerful access privileges that could allow circumvention of existing controls, and security reports used to monitor and identify unauthorized access to the system are cumbersome and virtually useless to managers for monitoring activity.

— In March 1995, the Office of Personnel Management Inspector General reported that federal retirement program assets were "highly vulnerable to loss or misuse" because of electronic data processing weaknesses, primarily excessively broad user access privileges, related to systems that maintained 2.1 million annuitant files and generated $36 billion in benefit payments during fiscal year 1994.

Individual audit reports describe varying causes for specific weaknesses at individual agencies. However, our audits have shown that an underlying factor is poorly managed security programs that do not proactively and systematically assess risk, monitor the effectiveness of security controls, and respond to identified problems. Such programs are essential to ensure that management and technical controls, including actions to correct identified weaknesses, are effective on a continuing basis.

As part of its various efforts to explore and develop policies associated with a range of information security issues, in February 1996, OMB issued a revised version of its central guidance to agencies on developing an effective information security program. Like the previous version, issued in 1985. "Security of Federal Automated Information Resources," establishes a minimum set of management controls that are to be included in federal automated information security programs. These include assigning responsibility for security, developing a system security plan, screening and training individual users, assessing risk, planning for disasters and contingencies, and reviewing security safeguards at least every 3 years.

It also requires agencies to clearly define responsibilities and expected behaviour for all individuals with access to automated systems and to implement security incident response and reporting capabilities. OMB worked extensively with the National Institute of Standards and Technology, agency security managers Written comments submitted by numerous organizations and individuals and the remarks of agency officials that GAO interviewed indicate that the revised guidance is generally considered to be a valuable and necessary update that recognizes the increasingly open and interconnected computer systems that support agency operations.

Comprehensive oversight requires independently identifying management issues, focusing attention on these issues, and ensuring appropriate resolution of identified problems. Policy analysts in OMB's Office of Information and Regulatory Affairs and program examiners in OMB's Resource Management Offices have monitored selected security issues at individual agencies. However, the scope and depth of efforts intended to uncover critical information security issues vary among agencies, and these efforts are often reactive. GAO met with OMB program examiners for 11 agencies.

Of these, examiners for eight agencies essentially reacted to recognized problems, saying that they had little expertise regarding information resource management and related security issues. They said that they only considered security when it was raised as a significant issue by agency managers or auditors and, then, usually as it pertained to a specific program or system. Examiners for two other agencies had taken a somewhat more proactive look at the agencies' automated operations, including security; while the examiner for the remaining agency said that program examiners almost never considered systems-related issues, including security, as part of their examinations.

As for focusing on management issues, although OMB's revision of Circular A-130 focused general attention on the importance of information security programs, OMB has not systematically monitored compliance with its guidance or the effectiveness of security programs at individual agencies, even though problems in several agencies have been reported for years. While analysts in OMB's Office of Information and Regulatory Affairs have gained a high-level understanding of agency programs through informal discussions with agency personnel, most program examiners, who usually obtain more detailed information about individual agency operations, generally do not consider the effectiveness of an agency's overall information security program.

OMB obtains little documented information to help it proactively oversee agency information security programs. It has routinely obtained agency annual internal control assessments required under the Federal Managers Financial Integrity Act and Strategic Information Resource Management Plans. However, these documents vary significantly in level of detail regarding security issues and are often of little value for overseeing security practices. OMB generally does not obtain the more detailed self assessments of information security that agencies should be using as the basis for these summaries.

OMB program examiners cited independent audit reports as one of their most useful sources of information because they provided an independent assessment of agency operations. However, in the past, independent audits of computer security have not routinely been performed for all major agencies. Audits performed under the CFO Act of 1990 promise to make such independent audit information more routinely available because, in practice, such audits generally include evaluating and testing controls over information security. In the early 1990s, selected segments of federal operations became subject to annual financial statement audits under the Act, and in 1994, this audit requirement was extended to all major federal entities by the Government Management Reform Act. As a result, the percentage of federal expenditures that is audited has been steadily growing, and is expected to reach 98 percent by fiscal year 1997.

However, significant aspects of some agencies' operations, such as those involving sensitive medical records, are not likely to be covered by financial statement audits. For this reason, it is important for OMB, as well as agency managers, to coordinate their reviews of CFO Act audit reports and their reviews of other types of information security assessments, such as self assessments. When viewed together, these audits and assessments may provide a more comprehensive view of agency information security and allow OMB and agency officials to identify gaps in review coverage.

In light of the growing significance of information security and the widespread reported weaknesses, it is essential that OMB take advantage of all opportunities to leverage its resources and take advantage of available information. In this regard, OMB can analyse the increasing amount of audit information that is becoming available due to recently expanded requirements for annual financial statement audits of federal agencies, under the CFO Act. Although CFO Act audits pertain primarily to financial management systems, OMB's Office of Information and Regulatory Affairs and Office of Federal Financial Management could use them, in conjunction with agency self assessments, to determine if all key systems had been reviewed at an individual agency and to monitor actions to correct reported information security problems.

Also, the recently established CIO Council can serve as a forum for addressing government wide information security issues, raising security awareness, and developing a strategic approach to better understanding the security problems facing federal agencies and improving federal information security programs. The Council, established in July 1996 through Executive Order, is intended to be "the principal interagency forum to improve agency practices on such matters as the design, modernization, use, sharing, and performance of agency information resources." It is chaired by OMB's Deputy Director for Management, and its membership includes CIOs at all major federal agencies.

To enhance OMB's ability to oversee and improve federal information security programs, GAO is making the following recommendations to the Director of OMB:

— Advocate and promote the CIO Council's adopton of information security as one of its top priorities and development of a strategic plan for (1) increasing awareness of the importance of information security, especially among senior agency executives, and (2) improving information security program management government wide. Initiatives that the CIO Council should consider incorporating in its strategic plan include;

— developing information on the existing security risks associated with nonclassified systems currently in use;

— developing information on the risks associated with evolving practices, such as Internet use;

— identifying best practices regarding information security programs so that they can be adopted by federal agencies;

— establishing a program for reviewing the adequacy of individual agency information security programs using interagency teams of reviewers;

— ensuring adequate review coverage of agency information security practices by considering the scope of various types of audits and reviews performed and acting to address any identified gaps in coverage;

— developing or identifying training and certification programs that can be shared among agencies; and

Identifying proven security tools and techniques.

—Direct the Office of Information and Regulatory Affairs, the Office of Federal Financial Management, and the Resource Management Offices to (1) supplement their current reviews of audit reports to include reviewing audits conducted under the CFO Act in order to identify any findings related to information security and (2) use this information, in conjunction with reports on agency self assessments, to assist in proactively monitoring the scope of such reviews and the effectiveness of agency information security practices.

— Encourage the development of improved sources of information with which to monitor compliance with OMB's guidance and the effectiveness of agency information security programs. This could include engaging assistance from private contractors or others with appropriate expertise, such as federally funded research and development centers.

— Direct the Office of Information and Regulatory Affairs to develop and implement a program for increasing program examiners' understanding of information security management issues so that they can more readily identify and understand the implications of information security weaknesses on agency programs.

Agency Comments and Evaluation

In written comments on a draft of this report, OMB agreed that information security is an important management issue and stated that certain of the report's recommendations are meritorious. In particular, OMB said that it will encourage the CIO Council to adopt information security as one of its top priorities and that it will review (1) the training and related materials provided to program examiners and (2) the availability of improved sources of information. However, OMB disagreed with the report's tone, which it characterized as suggesting "that OMB has not been dedicating sufficient resources in the past to overseeing the agencies' information security activities, and that therefore OMB in the future should dedicate more of its resources to this objective." In addition, OMB stated its concern that the report overemphasizes OMB's role and that this could distract federal agencies from their responsibilities as the primary managers of federal information security.

GAO agrees that agency managers are primarily responsible for information security. GAO's audit efforts related to information security over the past few years have focused almost exclusively on individual agency practices, and it has made dozens of related recommendations to agency officials. Thirty products resulting from this work and containing these recommendations are listed at the end of this report. The results of this work led GAO to identify a pattern of government wide information security weaknesses.

In light of the pattern of weaknesses that GAO has identified and the increasing importance of information security in virtually every aspect of federal operations, OMB has a vital leadership role to play in promoting and overseeing agency security practices. This role was recently reemphasized in the Information Technology Management Reform Act of 1996 and in revisions to the Paperwork Reduction Act, which together explicitly outline OMB's responsibilities for over seeing agency practices regarding information privacy and security. Information security has become a consideration in the management of virtually every major federal program and in billions of dollars in annual information technology investment decisions. For these reasons, GAO believes that information security, as well as other information management issues, merits a high priority relative toot her budget and management issues.

In this regard, GAO's recommendations are focused primarily not on increasing the amount of OMB resources but on increasing the impact of OMB's current resources by taking advantage of newly available audit information, discussed in chapter 4, and by expanding staff expertise. These actions, at a minimum, are needed to help address growing concerns over the adequacy of federal information security. GAO also believes that periodic oversight reviews of agency information security programs would be beneficial but that such reviews could be performed by interagency teams under the auspices of the OMB-chaired CIO Council.

As federal agencies expand their use of information technology, they face an increasing challenge to protect the integrity, confidentiality, and availability of information that is vital totheir missions. Like the nation as a whole, our government is becoming increasingly dependent on widely interconnected computer systems and the electronic data they maintain. These systems and data are essential to carry out critical operations, such as tax collections; safeguard billions of dollars in assets, such as military equipment and accounts receivable; and deliver basic services, such as social security payments and other benefits. Reliance on these systems and on electronic data is revolutionizingthe way that agencies collect, process, store, and disseminate information. However, without effective controls, such reliance also can increase the risks of financial loss, unauthorized access to sensitive information, and devastating interruptions in service.

To provide a government wide overview, this report summarizes the results of our reviews of information security at individual agencies and of similar assessments performed by others. The report also describes OMB's oversight of federal agency practices regarding information security and identifies opportunities for improvement. We performed this review in response to a request from Senator John Glenn, Ranking Minority Member, Senate Committee on Governmental Affairs, that we examine a broad range of federal information security issues. Subsequently, Senator Ted Stevens, Committee Chairman, also expressed interest in these issues.

Information security is a growing concern because the federal government, like the nation as a whole, is becoming increasingly dependent on computerized information systems and electronic records. These systems and records are fast replacing manual procedures and paper documents, which in many cases are no longer available as" backup" if automated systems should fail. The potential risks associated with reliance on electronic systems and records are exacerbated because more and more systems are being interconnected to form networks or are accessible through public telecommunication systems, making the systems themselves and the data they maintain much more difficult to protect from unauthorized users or outside intruders.

All major agencies rely on computer systems to provide critical support for their operations, and even greater reliance is planned for the future. In addition, agencies are increasing their use of inter connected systems and electronically transmitted data in order to streamline operations, make federally maintained data more accessible, and reduce paperwork.

Most notably, the Department of Defense has a vast information infrastructure that includes 2.1 million computers, 10,000 local networks, and 100 long-distance networks. The majority of the information maintained on Defense's computers is sensitive but non classified data essential to daily operations, such as commercial transactions; payroll, personnel, and health records; operational plans; and weapons systems maintenance records. In addition, Defense uses the Internet, a global network interconnecting thousands of computer networks, to exchange electronic mail, log on to remote computer sites, and obtain files from remote locations.

Civilian agencies are also increasingly reliant on interconnected systems, including the Internet, and on electronic data. The following examples illustrate just a few of the ways that agencies are expanding their use of information technology to support critical operations.

— Law enforcement officials throughout the United States and Canada rely on the Federal Bureau of Investigation's National Crime Information Center computerized database for access to sensitive criminal justice records on individual offenders. According to the Bureau's fiscal year 1997 budget submission, the system is available to 78,000 authorized users and processes an average of about 2 million transactions daily.

— The Internal Revenue Service (IRS), which relies on computers to process and store millions of taxpayer records, views electronic filing of tax returns as fundamental to its future operations. The number of individual income tax returns filed electronically increased from 4.2 million in 1990 to about 14.8 million for the first 3 and a half months of 1996. IRS goals include significantly increasing the number of electronically filed returns and eventually eliminating paper returns for a large segment of filers.

— The Customs Service relies on automated systems to process entry declarations, which totaled over 39 million in fiscal year 1994 and led to payment of over $20 billion in duties. Although many entry declarations are submitted as paper documents, a growing number are submitted electronically.

— The Department of Agriculture is reducing the use of paper food stamp coupons through its electronic benefits transfer program. Under the program, individual recipients' monthly benefits are recorded in a central computer file. Individuals then use "credit card" type cards with secret personal identification numbers to draw on these benefits and pay for their groceries. During fiscal year 1995, about

630,000 households participated in the electronic benefit transfer food stamp program. According to the Federal Electronic Benefits Transfer Task Force, the program could potentially cover over 10 million households.

— Medicare part B claims that were submitted and processed electronically jumped from 36 to 72 percent between 1990 and 1994, and further increases are likely. Medicare part B covers physician services, outpatient hospital care, medical supplies, and other health benefits, such as emergency ambulance service. The program cost $60 billion in fiscal year 1994, and, according to OMB, costs are expected to double over the subsequent 7 years.

Unfortunately, the same factors that are so important to streamlining federal operations—interconnected, often widely-dispersed systems; readily accessible information; and paperless processing—are also factors which increase the vulnerability of these operations and data. Specifically, the threats to agency systems and the potential for harm have increased because

— the move to more interconnected systems has provided greater numbers of individuals access to extensive databases of information through widely distributed networks of computers;

— agencies are placing greater reliance on electronic records, in some cases eliminating paper records; and

— intruders, including criminals, are becoming more skilled at defeating security techniques designed to protect computer systems and electronic information.

When systems are not adequately protected the potential for malicious and criminal acts is enormous. For example, by obtaining access to data files, an individual could make unauthorized changes for personal gain, such as diverting payments or reducing amounts owed on debts. Similarly, an individual could obtain sensitive information about business transactions or individuals, which could then be sold or used for malicious purposes. By obtaining access to computer programs, an individual could make unauthorized changes to these programs, which in turn could be used to access data files or to process unauthorized transactions, such as improper payments. Also, an intruder could eliminate evidence of unauthorized activity, thus, significantly reducing the likelihood that such activity would ever be detected.

Further, in an inadequately protected network environment, an agency's operations could be sabotaged from remote locations by altering or destroying critical data and programs, or by introducing malicious code, such as viruses, to damage or congest system operations. Significant damage could also occur as a result of accidental errors and deletions by authorized users. Regardless of the individual user's intent, in today's high-speed, highly automated, and interconnected computing environment, thousands of transactions could be erroneously processed or enormous amounts of data could be destroyed or disclosed before an agency detected the damage.

In addition to access control risks, computer facilities andelectronic media can be damaged or otherwise rendered unusable by fires, floods, contamination, and other man made and natural disasters. If an agency does not have adequate contingency plans and preparations for such unexpected events, it may be forced to suspend critical operations or it could lose data and software that are difficult and costly, or even impossible, to replace.

The need to protect sensitive federal data maintained on automated systems has been recognized for years in various laws and in federal guidance. The Privacy Act of 1974, as amended; the Paperwork Reduction Act of 1980, as amended; and the Computer Security Act of 1987 all contain provisions requiring agencies to protect the confidentiality and integrity of the sensitive information that they maintain. The Computer Security Act definessensitive information as "any information, the loss, misuse, or unauthorized access to or modification of which could adversely affect the national interest or the conduct of Federal programs, or the privacy to which individuals are entitled under the Privacy Act, but which has not been specifically authorized under criteria established by an Executive Order or an Act of Congress to be kept secret in the interest of national defense or foreign policy."

The adequacy of controls over computerized data is also addressed indirectly by the Federal Managers Financial Integrity Act (FMFIA) of 1987 (31 U.S.C. 3512(b) and (c)) and the Chief Financial Officers (CFO) Act of 1990. FMFIA requires agency managers to annually evaluate their internal control systems and report to the President and the Congress any material weaknesses that could lead to fraud, waste, and abuse in government operations. The CFO Act requires agency CFOs to develop and maintain financial management systems that provide complete, reliable, consistent, and timely information. Under the act, major federal agencies annually issue audited financial statements. In practice, such audits generally include evaluating and testing controls over information security.

In accordance with the Paperwork Reduction Act of 1980, OMB is responsible for developing information security policies and overseeing agency practices. In this regard, OMB has provided guidance for agencies in OMB Circular A-130. Security of Federal Automated Information Resources." Since 1985, this circular has directed agencies to implement an adequate level of security for all automated information systems that ensures (1) effective and accurate operations and (2) continuity of operations for systems that support critical agency functions. The circular establishes a minimum set of controls to be included in federal agency information system security programs and requires agencies to review system security at least every 3 years.

Responsibility for developing technical standards and providing related guidance for sensitive data belongs primarily to the National Institute of Standards and Technology (NIST), under the Computer Security Act.OMB, NIST, and agency responsibilities regarding information security were recently reemphasized in the Information Technology Management Reform Act of 1996.

Our objectives were to (1) provide a general overview of the adequacy of federal information security at major federal agencies based on reported information, (2) identify and categorize the most significant information security weaknesses reported, (3) identify the general causes of reported weaknesses, and (4) assess OMB' efforts to oversee agency information security practices. Toaccomplish these objectives we analyzed the results of our evaluations of computer-related controls at five major agencies since June 1993.

These agencies included the Internal Revenue Service and the U.S. Customs Service, which are both part of the Department of the Treasury; the Department of Education; the Department of the Army; and the Department of Housing and Urban Development. Weper formed most of these assessments as part of our financial statement audits at these agencies. While such audits focus on the security of the data supporting the financial statements, they include evaluations and tests of general controls that affect a significant segment of the agencies' computerized operations.

A list of GAO reports and testimonies that address the adequacy of information security at federal agencies is provided at the end of this report. We supplemented reviews of our own audits with an analysis of 149 other reports on major federal agencies to determine if information security weaknesses had been reported and, if so, what types of weaknesses were reported. The reports we reviewed resulted from independent audits by agency inspectors general issued between September 1992 through March 1996, and from agency self assessments required under FMFIA for fiscal years 1994 and 1995. The agencies covered included the Departments of Agriculture, Defense, Education, Energy, Health and Human Services, Housing and Urban Development, Justice, Labor, Transportation, the Treasury, and Veterans Affairs; the General Services Administration; the National Aeronautics and Space Administration; the Social Security Administration; and the Office of Personnel Management. Together, our analyses covered the 15 major departments and agencies that are responsible for spending or safeguarding the largest amounts of federal resources. In total, these agencies accounted for over 98 percent of all federal outlays during fiscal year 1995.

We based our analyses almost exclusively on reported findings. Although we spoke with inspector general audit managers at several agencies to clarify information that had been reported, we did not assess the quality or completeness of any of the inspector general audits or agency self assessments covered by our survey.

To augment information included in reports on individual agencies, we met with members of the steering committee of the Federal Computer Security Managers Forum, an information-sharing group established by NIST, and we reviewed various OMB and NIST documents, as well as related laws.

To obtain information on OMB's oversight efforts, we met with officials from OMB's Office of Information and Regulatory Affairs (OIRA), Office of Federal Financial Management, and Resource Management Office branches responsible for overseeing programs at 11 of the 15 agencies included in our review. In addition, we met with senior information resource management officials and security program managers at five agencies to discuss their interactions with OMB and other agencies responsible for providing guidance and assistance regarding information security issues. These five agencies are the Departments of Agriculture, Health and Human Services, Treasury, and Transportation and the Office of Personnel Management.

Our review was performed in Washington, D.C., from July 1995 through May 1996 in accordance with generally accepted government auditing standards. We requested written comments on a draft of this report from the Acting Director of OMB or his designee. OMB's Deputy Director for Management provided written comments on a draft of this report. These comments are discussed in the "Agency Comments and Our Evaluation" sect. Recent audits show that weak information security is a serious government wide problem that is putting major federal operations at risk.

Between September 1994 and April 30, 1996, serious weaknesses were reported for two-thirds of the agencies covered by our review, and for half of these agencies the weaknesses had been reported for at least 5 years. A fundamental cause of these weaknesses is that agencies have not implemented security programs that provide as systematic means of assessing risk, implementing effective policies and control techniques, and monitoring the effectiveness of these policies and techniques.

Of the 15 agencies included in our review, serious information security control weaknesses were reported for 10 from September 1994 through April 1996. The two most commonly reported weakness indicate fundamental deficiencies in the ability of agencies to protect federal information and the continuity of federal operations. The first was poor access control, which increases the risk that an individual or group could inappropriately modify or disclose sensitive data or computer programs for purposes such as personal gain or sabotage. The second most commonly reported weakness was inadequate disaster planning, which increases the risk that an agency will not be able to satisfactorily recover from an unexpected interruption in critical operations. Many of the identified weaknesses have remained uncorrected for years. Of the 10 agencies with reported weaknesses, FMFIA reports for 5 showed that the problems had remained uncorrected for 5 years or longer.

Examples of reported problems include the following:

— Estimates by the Department of Defense indicate that attacks on unclassified computer systems and networks are a serious and growing threat to our national security, including Defense's ability to execute military operations and protect sensitive information. Defense data indicate that Defense may have experienced as many as 250,000 attacks in 1995 and that the number of attacks is doubling each year. Successful attacks by outside intruders have shut down systems and corrupted sensitive data. However, estimates based on tests conducted since 1992 showed that less than 1 percent of attacks on Defense's systems were detected and reported. Although no summary costs have been developed, Defense officials estimate that the cost of such incidents is at least tens of millions of dollars per year.

— During our audit of the IRS' fiscal year 1995 financial statements, we found that, as reported since 1993, controls over sensitive information were inadequate.

Although corrective actions are under way, as detailed in previousreports, IRS could not ensure that the confidentiality and accuracy of taxpayer data were protected and that the data were not manipulated for purposes of individual gain. Specifically, (1) controls did not prevent users from unauthorized access to sensitive programs and data files, (2) numerous users were allowed powerful access privileges that could allow circumvention of existing controls, and (3) security reports used to monitor and identify unauthorized access to the system were cumbersome and virtually useless to managers for monitoring activity. In addition, back-up and recovery plans were inadequate to provide reasonable assurance that IRS service centers could recover from disasters.

In June 1994, we reported a variety of computer-related control weaknesses at the Customs Service, including that thousands of internal and external users had inappropriate access to critical and sensitive programs and data files. In May 1995, the Department of the Treasury Inspector General reported that despite attempts to correct the problem, the weaknesses continued to exist.

— In June 1994 and June 1995, we reported that controls over the Department of Education's Federal Family Education Loan Program (FFELP) did not adequately protect sensitive data files, application programs, and systems software from unauthorized access, change, or disclosure. These controls are critical to Education's ability to safeguard FFELP assets, maintain sensitive loan data, and ensure the reliability of financial management information about the program. The Department reported that FFELP had $77 billion in outstanding loan guarantees as of September 30, 1994.

— The Department of Health and Human Services (HHS) first reported the lack of a formal, well-coordinated system security program in its Administration for Children and Families in its fiscal year 1990 FMFIA report. In December 1995, HHS reported that the Administration still had not implemented fundamental computer security program elements such as risk assessments and independent reviews of contingency plans for sensitive systems supporting this $17 billion dollar per year program.

— The Department of Justice first recognized automated data processing security as a weakness in 1985.

Although Justice reported in February 1996 that it has made department wide security improvements, it also reported that some components had not completed and tested continuity of operations plans, developed policies for computer and telecommunications security, or conducted required risk assessments of component computer systems.

— In March 1995, the Department of Agriculture's Inspector General reported that controls over access to computer software programs and data were inadequate to prevent unauthorized activity at the Department's National Finance Center. The Center processes billions of dollars in payments and sensitive information for itself and other agencies, including payroll, retirement savings, administrative and travel payments, and property management information.

— In March 1995, the Office of Personnel Management Inspector General reported that federal retirement program assets were "highly vulnerable to loss or misuse" because of electronic data processing weaknesses, primarily excessively broad user access privileges, related to systems that maintained 2.1 million annuitant files and generated $36 billion in benefit payments during fiscal year 1994.

Serious information security weaknesses may also exist for some of the five agencies for which no weaknesses were reported. This is because audit reports at one agency specifically stated that computer-related controls had not been reviewed as part of the audit. Also, audit managers at two other agencies said that their computer audit capabilities were limited, and they could not readily determine what, if any, work they or their contractors had performed in this area.

For the 10 agencies with serious reported weaknesses, auditors made 90 new recommendations for specific corrective actions in reports issued from September 1994 through May 1996. In addition, these reports referred to numerous recommendations made in prior years that had not yet been fully or effectively implemented.

Although most agencies have reported actions initiated or planned to correct their weaknesses, a recurring condition reported in GAO, inspector general, and FMFIA reports is that agency actions, while resulting in some improvement, are not completed promptly and do not adequately address identified problems. Recent audits at IRS, Education, and Customs all found that, while some improvements had been made, corrective actions at those agencies had been repeatedly delayed or were incomplete.

As with Defense, the costs of agencies' information security weaknesses cannot be determined because agencies generally do not keep summary records of security violations or account for the cost of responding to such violations. In addition, due to poor controls and lack of user awareness, it is possible that many violations are not being detected or reported.

Security Programme Management

A well designed and managed security program with senior-level support is essential for ensuring that an agency's controls are appropriate and effective on a continuing basis. In this regard, managing information security is similar to managing risks associated with other aspects of agency operations. The program should establish a process and assign responsibilities for systematically (1) assessing risk, (2) promoting user awareness of security issues, (3) developing and implementing effective security policies and related control techniques, (4) monitoring the appropriateness and effectiveness of these policies and techniques, and (5) providing feedback to managers who may then make adjustments as needed. Such a program can provide senior officials a means of managing information security risks and the related costs rather than just reacting to individual incidents.

Without a well designed and managed program, security controls may be inadequate; responsibilities may be unclear, misunderstood, and improperly implemented; and controls may be ineffective or inconsistently applied. Such conditions generally result in insufficient protection of sensitive or critical resources and, conversely, may result in disproportionately high expenditures for controls over low-risk resources.

Individual audit reports describe varying causes for specific control weaknesses at individual agencies. However, in our reviews of information security controls, we found that the major underlying factor was lack of a well managed information security program with senior management support. For example, in May 1996, we reported that Defense had not established a comprehensive computer security program and had not assigned responsibility for ensuring that such a program was implemented. As a result, Defense information security policies were dated, inconsistent, and incomplete; user awareness was insufficient; and security personnel were inadequately trained.

Similarly, in August 1995, we reported that IRS had no proactive, independent information security group that was systematically deployed to review the adequacy and consistency of security over IRS' computer operations. Instead, IRS was addressing information security issues on a reactive basis. In June 1995, we reported that information security weaknesses at Education resulted from the Department's overall weak security administration and failure to develop and implement key policies and procedures. Several of the inspector general audit reports that we reviewed also indicated that agency managers were not taking the steps needed to ensure that controls had been implemented and were operating properly.

To gain an additional perspective on the causes of poor controls, we met with selected members of the steering committee of the Federal Computer Security Managers Forum, an information-sharing group established by NIST. These officials said that additional support from senior management would allow them to establish more effective programs. According to forum members, a lack of management support can result in inadequate resources devoted to information security, a situation that limits the ability of security program managers to address security needs proactively.

A number of factors can contribute to the perception of a lack of senior management support for information security. First, as with other types of internal controls, senior managers may view security efforts as impediments to the efficient accomplishment of the agency's mission. This is because security controls cost money to implement and monitor, and, generally, they diminish the ease with which systems and data can be accessed and updated.

In addition, some senior managers may be unaware of the full range of threats and vulnerabilities that must be considered when determining what level of information security is adequate. Others may not have the data they need to make informed decisions. As a result, they may want to adopt information technology for new applications without adequately considering the related risks, or they may be unwilling to strengthen security over existing procedures.

A comprehensive security program can help senior managers maintain an appropriate balance between operational efficiency and security by systematically and continually fine-tuning policies and control procedures through a risk assessment, monitoring, and feedback cycle. As agency systems become more interconnected and open to large numbers of outside users and as more sophisticated technical controls become available, the effort needed to manage agency systems and monitor the effectiveness of related controls will become more complex and more time-consuming. The benefits of better service and lower processing costs should far outweigh the cost of these additional security efforts. However, it will be important for senior managers to recognize the security challenges involved and to help their organizations successfully meet these challenges. OMB has participated in a variety of efforts to develop government wide policies regarding federal information security, and it recently issued an updated version of its central guidance to agencies on minimum automated information security program requirements.

OMB has also monitored agency efforts to address recognized security weaknesses or potential weaknesses related to individual agency programs or systems.

However, OMB has not proactively attempted to identify and address the underlying causes of these problems, which often are rooted in the design and management of an agency's overall information security program. In addition, the depth and scope of OMB's monitoring efforts have varied significantly from one agency to another.

Although security program management is primarily the responsibility of agency managers, under the Paperwork Reduction Act, OMB is charged with overseeing the use of federal information resources, including providing direction and overseeing the "privacy, confidentiality, security, disclosure, and sharing of information." OMB oversees and guides agency operations through its three statutory offices, which are primarily responsible for setting policy, and its five Resource Management Offices (RMO). which are primarily responsible for examining agency budget issues and overseeing agencies implementation of government wide management policies. The Office of Information and Regulatory Affairs (OIRA) is the statutory office responsible for establishing government wide information resource management policies, including those related to information security, and assisting the RMOs in overseeing agency implementation of these policies.

OIRA's information security oversight efforts are conducted primarily by its Information Policy and Technology Branch, which employs 10 individuals who regularly deal with government wide information resource management issues. Three of these individuals haveroutinely spent a significant amount of their time on information security issues.

Over the last few years the Branch has participated in various projects to address cross-cutting information security issues as part of its overall responsibility to establish information resource Management policies. These include efforts to (1) develop federal policies on the use of cryptography, (2) define the federal role regarding the security of the national information infrastructure. assist the General Services Administration in developing telecommunications security requirements, and (4) explore security issues related to electronic commerce. However, the Branch's most basic and comprehensive accomplishment regarding federal agency security practices was developing an updated version of OMB Circular A-130.

Issued in February 1996, to clarify guidance to agencies on managing information security as they increasingly rely on open and interconnected systems. Like the previous version, issued in 1985, establishes a minimum set of controls that are to be included in federal automated information security programs. These include assigning responsibility for security, developing a system security plan, screening and training individual users, assessing risk, planning for disasters and contingencies, and reviewing security safeguards at least every 3 years. It also requires agencies to clearly define responsibilities and expected behaviour for all individuals with access to automated systems and to implement security incident response and reporting capabilities.

OIRA obtained significant input from agency managers, NIST, and the Computer System Security and Privacy Advisory Board, including written comments from over 27 organizations and individuals, before issuing the final version. The senior information resource managers and security program managers that we met also generally agreed that OIRA had done a good job of developing and communicating guidance regarding information security and responding to their individual requests for clarification of guidance. To assist in overseeing agency practices regarding information resource management, including security, analysts in OIRA's Information Policy and Technology Branch communicate frequently with RMO program examiners to (1) help ensure that the examiners are aware of high-risk or problem areas that affect the agency programs and (2) provide technical assistance to the RMOs, sometimes at the request of individual examiners.

The Branch also attempts to maintain an understanding of agency practices through informal discussions with agency personnel and participation in various conferences and meetings. For example, the Branch's primary information security policy analyst estimates that he has made six to eight presentations at individual agencies per year and numerous presentations at professional conferences and meetings, such as those of the Computer System Security and Privacy Advisory Board. He has also routinely participated in the Federal Computer Security Managers Forum, which is sponsored by NIST and meets approximately every 4 to 6 weeks. At Forum meetings, he has the opportunity to talk directly with the individuals who are responsible for administering agency security programs.

However, OIRA does not systematically monitor agency compliance with OMB information security guidance or assess the effectiveness of agency information security management practices that are fundamental elements in the agencies' ability to effectively deal with information security risks and identified weaknesses.

The most recent effort to methodically gain a relatively detailed overview of agency practices was completed in 1992. That effort involved a series of visits at each of 28 agencies by a team of OMB, NIST, and National Security Agency representatives. According to a January 1992 letter to the Director of OMB from the Computer System Security and Privacy Advisory Board, the visits were enthusiastically received and resulted in greater awareness on the part of senior officials, which, in turn, resulted in increased management support for agency computer security programs.

Despite the apparent success of the 1992 visits, Information Policy and Technology Branch officials said that they have no plans to repeat the effort because it was very resource intensive. They said that as a result, no systematic visits to agencies were currently planned and that any future efforts along this line would address a range of information resource management concerns in addition to security.

Engaging the services of contractors on a limited basis would be one means by which OMB could supplement its staff resources and periodically take a closer look at individual agency practices. Information Policy and Technology Branch officials told us that OMB has not customarily used contractors to assist in carrying out its oversight responsibilities. At GAO, we have found that engaging contractors to assist on individual projects can be a cost-effective means of expanding our ability to review agency operations, especially in areas such as information security where very specific and often highly technical expertise may be needed.

Information Security Practices

We met with branch chiefs and program examiners responsible for examining programs at 11 of the 15 agencies covered by our review and found that their attention to information security varied. Examiners for all but one agency said that they considered information security during their examination of agency budgets and programs to some extent, although examiners for eight agencies said that they only did so when it had been highlighted by agency management or in audit reports as a problem. These considerations were generally limited to monitoring agency progress in correcting recognized problems and did not involve examining an agency's information security program or the effectiveness of agency security practices in general. For example, the RMO branches overseeing the Departments of Agriculture and Education and the Office of Personnel Management all said that they had paid special attention to security issues associated with certain systems or facilities because weaknesses had been recently reported.

The program examiners and their branch chiefs said that information security is usually not closely examined because it is only one of many issues demanding their attention. The number of program examiners responsible for each agency varied from about 5 for the Department of Education to about 30 for the Department of Defense.

There were a few cases where known problems were receiving virtually no attention from the RMOs. Most notably, the representative that we spoke with about the branches that oversee the Department of Defense said that the program examiners there almost never considered problems related to information systems, including security, because such issues did not seem to have a significant budget impact compared to other issues and programs. He emphasized that due to the Department of Defense's size and variety of programs, the Defense examiners had to be very selective in deciding which items merited examination. Also, a long-standing problem regarding a lack of disaster recovery planning at the Department of Veterans Affairs (VA) appeared to have prompted little interest from the RMO branch responsible for overseeing the Department, although other security issues were considered.

Officials in several branches indicated that they were becoming increasingly sensitized to the significance of information security due to recent operational issues within their agencies. For example, the VA Branch Chief said that VA's efforts to streamline its processes by accessing needed information in other agencies' systems had raised a number of concerns about the security of shared data and the related legal requirements. Similar concerns were expressed by the branches overseeing system modernization projects at the Department of Agriculture and the Health Care Financing Administration because these projects would result in increased accessibility of sensitive information on individuals.

Despite the increasing importance of information security, few of the program examiners said that they had any significant experience or expertise in dealing with information systems or related security issues. Most said that due to their lack of expertise, they depended largely on OIRA to help them understand the issues and assess related agency actions. Most of the branches said they had good working relationships with OIRA, as well as the other statutory offices within OMB, and that when they needed technical assistance, it was available. Also, some branches had informally designated an individual with some experience in examining systems-related issues to review these issues and to serve as a resource for other examiners in the branch.

Two of the branches we visited each had a relatively experienced individual to assist in the branch's examinations. These individuals were very familiar with their agencies' information processing operations and appeared to have performed a much more comprehensive review of information security than had been performed by other branches.

OMB provides no formal training to the RMO program examiners regarding information systems management and related security issues. Each summer, OMB provides several days of seminars on issues of interest to examiners. However, only a few hours are devoted to topics handled by OIRA, including information resource management issues, such as system development issues and security.

Officials in the Information Policy and Technology Branch believe that ad hocon-the-job learning is more effective in increasing the expertise of program examiners than a more formal program of training or awareness sessions would be. This is because the examiners can be overwhelmed by the volume of information available to them, and they are more likely to absorb information that is immediately useful. However, one branch chief said that there are few on-the-job learning opportunities regarding security issues because his branch devotes little attention to such issues.

To effectively oversee and influence any activity, it is essential to have meaningful, reliable, and routinely available information on the operations being examined. However, the documented information that OMB routinely obtains on the design and effectiveness of agency information security programs varies significantly in quality, quantity, and usefulness.

Officials in OIRA's Information Policy and Technology Branch said that they routinely obtain annual internal control assessments required under the Federal Managers' Financial Integrity Act (FMFIA) and strategic information resource management plans. Since 1985, OMB Circular A-130. Also, the Computer Security Act requires each agency to include a summary of its information security plan in its strategic information resource management plan that it submits annually to OMB. However, these documents vary significantly in level of detail and were of ten of little value for oversight purposes.

Our review found that the FMFIA reports tended to contain very cursory information that made it difficult to precisely understand the nature of the weakness reported. Similarly, most of the security program summaries were very brief, and, in most cases, they only described very general agency goals and policies, with little information on the effectiveness of the program or on planned improvements. Further, the reporting formats varied considerably among agencies.

The RMO branches that we met with said that they attempted to obtain whatever information was available on the programs they examined, in addition to the agency budget documents that were the starting point for their examinations. However, most RMO examiners said that they did not routinely seek out information on or review agency security programs and that any investigation of security issues that they made was almost always prompted by issues raised by management or auditors.

Most examiners said that they relied primarily on inquiries of agency officials and related documentation in examining agency programs, including any security issues that they were aware of. However, they also said that they used audit reports, usually issued by agency inspectors general and by GAO. Several examiners noted that such audit reports were useful both in providing them an independent assessment of agency operations and in strengthening their ability to encourage agency actions. Also, several of the branches said that their examinations benefitted from good working relationships with agency inspector general officials, who would alert them to key inspector general reports and other issues. We found that, for the most part, at least one examiner in each of the branches we met with was familiar with the information security weaknesses that had been reported in inspector general, GAO, and FMFIA reports for their agencies. However, some examiners were unaware of related detailed reports that had been issued on these weaknesses.

Until recently, independent audits of information security practices were performed largely at the discretion of inspector general offices and GAO and in response to congressional interest. As a result, OMB analysts and examiners could not rely on such reports being routinely available. However, program examiners at some agencies said that they have begun to review annual audits performed under the CFO Act as a means of monitoring agency control weaknesses, including those related to information security. These audits are discussed further in chapter 4 of this report.

Two relatively new developments can serve to improve and facilitate OMB's ability to oversee and influence the effectiveness of agency information security programs. One is an expansion of independent information security reviews prompted by financial statement audits required under the CFO Act. Another is the recently established CIO Council, which can serve as a forum for addressing government wide information security issues and raising security awareness.

Information Security Controls

Although Inspector General offices and GAO have reviewed information security at federal agencies on a selective basis for decades, audits performed under the CFO Act promise to make such independent audit information more routinely available at all major agencies. Generally, CFO Act audits are required to include an evaluation of the auditee 's internal controls, including information security controls. Such evaluations can assist OMB and the Congress in their oversight roles and serve as useful tools for agency managers.

In the early 1990s, selected segments of federal operations became subject to annual financial statement audits by agency inspect or general offices under the CFO Act. In 1994, this audit requirement was extended to all major federal entities by the Government Management Reform Act (Public Law 103-356). As a result, the percentage of federal expenditures that is audited has been steadily growing, and, by fiscal year 1997, about 98 percent will be covered by such audits.

The primary responsibility for monitoring information security programs rests with agency managers who must routinely assess their programs and adjust policies and practices as needed. However, independent audits, such as the CFO Act audits, can be useful to OMB because they provide an objective evaluation that may identify weaknesses that were overlooked by agency self assessments. For example, IRS did not report its information security weaknesses in its annual FMFIA report until after independent audits had identified the weaknesses.

Although the reviews of computer security controls associated with CFO Act audits pertain to financial management systems, they usually cover a significant portion of each agency's operations. This is because program and financial systems often are supported by common data centers and communications networks that are subject to the same general controls. For example, personnel responsible for makingneeded changes to software are likely to follow the same set of procedures for controlling such changes regardless of whether they pertain to a financial or non financial system.

Similarly, the adequacy of a disaster recovery plan for a large data center is likely to affect the security of all of that center's operations—both financial and non financial. Also, programmanagement systems often are the source of many detailed financial transactions and, therefore, are included in the auditor's review. However, there are significant aspects of some agencies' operations involving sensitive computerized data that are not likely to be covered by financial statement audits.

Examples include medical records and certain types of data supporting law enforcement operations. For this reason, it is important for OMB, as well as agency managers, to coordinate their reviews of CFO Act audit reports and their reviews of other information security assessments, such as self assessments conducted in accordance with FMFIA and OMB CircularA-130. When viewed together, these audits and assessments may provide a more comprehensive view of agency information security and allow OMB and agency officials to identify gaps in review coverage. The awareness and use of CFO Act audit reports as a means of identifying information security weaknesses varied among the OMB analysts and examiners that we spoke with. This is understandable since audits of many agency programs have not been required until recently, and the routine availability of annual financial audit reports is relatively new. OIRA officials told us that they had not viewed these reports as a source of information on agency compliance with federal policies, because they did not realize that information security reviews were generally included in financial statement audits.

However, they said that in the future, they would obtain CFO audit reports from OMB's Office of Federal Financial Management, where they are routinely received from agencies. The awareness of RMO program examiners was mixed. Most were aware of the CFO audit reports that affected the programs they were responsible for examining. However, a few were unaware of significant information security problems that had been reported.

Bibliography

Awade, Priscilla, "Planning for Disaster", *Information Age*, July/ August, 1997.

Barr A., Cohen P. R. and Feigenbaum E. A., *The Handbook of Artificial Intelligence*, 3 vols. Kaufmann, Los Altos, CA, 1981.

Bartram S., Gibson B., *Training Needs Analysis*, 2nd ed. Aldershot, Gower, 1997.

Brant, Irving, *The Bill of Rights: Its Origin and Meaning*, New York: New American Library, 1965.

Charles. R. McClure, John Carlo Bertot and Douglas L. Zweizing, *Public Libraries and Internet: Study Results, Policy Issues and Recommendations*, Washington, DC: National Commission on Library Information Science, 1994.

David K. Berninghausen, "Report of Intellectual Freedom Committee to Council, Dallas, June 25, 1971", *American Libraries* 2: 891, Sept. 1971.

Gallegos, Frederic, et al., *Audit and Control of Information Systems*, London, South-Western University Press, 1987.

Hayes J. E. and D. Michie (eds), *Intelligent Systems: The Unprecedented Opportunity* Ellis Horwood, Chichester, England, 1983.

Hentoff, Nat, *The First Freedom: The Tumultuous History of Free Speech in America*, New York, Delacorte Press, 1980.

Laine Farlely (ed.), *Library Resources on Internet: Strategies for Selection and Use*, Chicago: America Library Association, Reference and Adult Services Division, 1993.

Leigh Robert D., "Intellectual Freedom", *ALA Bulletin* 42: 369, Sept. 1948.

Nash Deanna C. and David A. Bollier, "Protecting Privacy in the Age of Hometech", *Technology Review*, August-September 1981.

Pool Ithiel de Sola, *Technologies of Freedom: On Free Speech in an Electronic Age* Harvard University Press, Cambridge, MA, 1983.

Simons G. L., *Privacy in the Computer Age* NCC, Manchester, England, 1982.

Waltz David L., "Artificial Intelligence," *Scientific American*, October 1982.

David. I. Bainbridge, 'Software copyrights', Butterworths Publications, 1999.

Gopalakrishnan. N.S, 'Intellectual property and Criminal Law', National Law School of India University, Bangalore, 1999.

Michael Edenbough, 'Intellectual Property Law', Cavendish Publishing Ltd., Great Britain 1995.

Rahul Mathan, 'The law relating to computers and Internet', Butterworths India, 2000.

Saffady, William *Electronic Document Imaging System: Design, Evaluation and Implementation*, Westport CT: Meckler, 1993.

Index